MW00522811

This Book Is Presented To

Angel

Presented By

Andrea Walker

Date Presented

1/5/99   _Enjoy!_

All The

Man

I Need

Black
Women's
Loving
Expressions
On The
Men They
Desire

All The Man I Need

Black Women's Loving Expressions On The Men They Desire

Anaezi Modu ∽ *Andrea Walker*

GATEWAY PUBLISHERS
Newark, New Jersey

Copyright © 1999 by Anaezi Modu and Andrea Walker. All rights reserved. No part of this book may be reproduced in any form, or by any means, without the permission of the publisher. Exceptions are to be made for brief excerpts to be used in published reviews.

Published by Gateway Publishers
P.O. Box 1749, Newark, NJ 07101

ISBN: 1-887646-04-3
Printed in the United States of America

The "Mr. Right" Contest, which provided the entries for this book, was neither sponsored nor endorsed by *Essence* magazine. The contest was sponsored by AB Communications. *Essence* magazine published the notice for the contest in its "Graffiti" section. *Essence* is a registered trademark of *Essence* Communications.

Publisher's Cataloging in Publication Data

Modu, Anaezi.
        All the man I need: black women's loving expressions
on the men they desire / Anaezi Modu, Andrea Walker. –
1st ed.
    p. cm
    Includes index.
    Preassigned LCCN: 98-96211
    ISBN: 1-887646-04-3

    1. Mate selection. 2. Afro-American women–Attitudes.
3. Interpersonal attraction. 4. Man-woman relationships.
I. Walker, Andrea. II. Title.

HQ801.M64 1998   646.7′7
                          QBI98-844

CONTENTS

ACKNOWLEDGEMENTS

Special thanks to everyone that responded to our announcement and shared their thoughts on the men they desire. We also give special thanks to Ms. Sherrill D. Clarke, *Essence* Senior Copy Editor, for helping us get the word out to the readers, to Arsene Eglise and Sophie Smith, for their help in editing and proofreading, and to Khalilah Sharif, Claudette Palmer and Blessing Nwele for their typing services. Thanks also to the librarians at the Newark Public Library for helping us in our research.

— Anaezi Modu & Andrea Walker

Thank you to my friends and family for their love, support, and able assistance on this and on my numerous projects. From those that received and helped sort the volumes of entries mailed to us, to those that helped with selecting and proofreading the entries included in the book. Special thanks to my parents, Dr. and Mrs. Christopher C. Modu for their relentless support and encouragement on all our endeavors. Special thanks also go to the tireless staff at Gateway Publishers for their commitment to putting out a final product of which we can all be proud.

— Anaezi Modu

I dedicate this book to my father, Arthur DeWitt Walker, Jr. who is forever cherished in my heart. To my husband, Manny: my lover, brother, best friend, and teacher. With you, I have come home. Thank-you for showing us how and insisting on excellence! I am proud of you and of our steps together. To Anaezi: thank-you for your creative mind, for helping us turn all our dreams to reality, and for always being there for us all. To my mother, Dr. Jeanne M. Walker: thank-you for the gift of shining tomorrows and your loving embrace. My deepest love and respect. To Dr. and Mrs. Christopher C. Modu: Papa and Mama, thank-you for your love, confidence in our abilities and never-ending support of our dreams. To Leslie, Melissa, Ijeoma, Enechi, Sophie, Chi, Aunt Retia and JaRee: you are extremely dear to me. Another step to all our dreams. For Nkem, Amara, Ikenna, Ijeoma, Anziya and Eugenia: our future and our six most precious gifts.

— Andrea Walker

To The Men and Women

... If Black women do not love, there is no love. As the women go, so go the people. Stopping the woman stops the future. If Black women do not love, strength disconnects, families sicken, growth is questionable, and there are few reasons to conquer ideas or foes. If Black men do not love, shouting starts, the shooting commences, boys fill prisons, and our women grow gardens off to themselves. If Black women and men love, so come flowers from sun, rainbows at dusk. As Black women and men connect, the earth expands, minds open and our yeses become natural as we seek HeartLove.

Haki R. Madhubuti
HeartLove: Wedding and Love Poems

One

Our Loving Ways

Much has been written about the qualities men look for in women. Rarely are women, especially Black women, asked to identify the qualities they value in men. *All The Man I Need* provides a forum for Black women to speak for themselves about the characteristics they cherish in men. It also gives women of all ages and all walks of life, the opportunity to reflect on their own expectations of men. In addition, this book is a resource to help men break the "love code" by learning what women truly desire in relationships.

We also envisioned *All The Man I Need* as a book to counter the all-too-frequent negative portrayal of relationships between Black men and women. We, as Black women, prefer to present a more positive view. We know our men. We know their strengths and their weaknesses. More importantly, we love them for the promise of what they can be when given the opportunity and when their spiritual compasses are intact.

Yes, we can criticize our men to ensure that they satisfy our needs. But it should be done with love and with the best of intentions. Adding to the already abundant chorus of negativity about our relationships distorts who we really are as a people.

The foundation for *All The Man I Need* was established when we asked women to participate in the "Mr. Right" Contest announced in *Essence* magazine. The contest invited the magazine's readers to share with us their views on their ideal men. From one small notice, tucked away in the *Graffiti* section of the magazine, came 1,850 submissions written by women between the ages of 16 and 72 from all over the country and abroad. Administrators, doctors, homemakers, lawyers, military personnel, postal workers, secretaries, teachers, and unemployed women eagerly shared their thoughts about their ideal men. Of the nearly two thousand women who submitted passages for the contest, the winning entry was written by Cassandre Genevieve Harper and can be found on page 92.

Whether sharing whimsical dreams or remaining grounded in reality, these women long for men with whom they can be happy, safe, and emotionally centered. They want men in their lives who respect them as co-partners in a loving relationship. Consider the top 10 qualities the women say they value in men:

1. spirituality and religious convictions;
2. kindness, gentleness, compassion, and sensitivity;

3. strength in character and dignity;
4. honesty, faithfulness, and commitment;
5. sensuality and romance;
6. ability to pamper, comfort, and protect;
7. respect for women (especially their mother);
8. a non-controlling nature, an unconditional lover;
9. family oriented; and
10. a sense of humor.

These qualities were ranked according to how frequently they were mentioned in the entries sent to us by the women that entered the "Mr. Right" Contest.

Some of these qualities, when taken as a whole, may seem to describe a hero from a paperback romance. To be sure, some women have spun wonderful dreams of magnificent, proud and loving Black men. Drop-dead gorgeous men who will mysteriously appear in their lives, ready to adore them and to untangle them from their emotional and financial problems.

Other women, however, remain grounded in reality. For them, the ten qualities listed above are common to good men, not necessarily chivalrous heroes. They write about men in their lives who already possess these characteristics. They share poignant experiences and recollections of husbands, fathers, and partners who have profoundly impacted their lives.

Chapters Two to Fourteen contain the reflections of the women that wrote us. We grouped these passages into broad categories of qualities the women look for in their men. Chapter Fifteen contains the Partner Assessment and Compatibility Test (PACT™) which is based on the collective wisdom of the women that responded to our contest. The PACT will help readers determine if their current or prospective partners are right for them. Chapter Sixteen contains demographic information about the 1,850 women who submitted their passages. Readers interested in further exploring Black male-female relationships, can log onto our website, *www.blackromantic.com.*

We invite you to journey with us to explore Black women's soulful expressions on their men. It's a loving and heart-warming journey paved with creative bouquets of thoughts that display a different side of Black love as you have never seen before in print. While we may have put a little polish on a phrase or two, we did not tamper with the spirit or the passion of the women's loving messages about Black men.

We are confident that in reading *All The Man I Need*, you will be captivated, proud, amused, and sometimes, simply tearful. We will now share with you, Black women's loving expressions on the men they desire...

Two

The Conscious Heart

Sensitive & Communicative | Compassionate & Not Abusive
Kind & Faithful | Honest & Humble | Sense of Humor

Men are often viewed as strong, fearless and aggressive creatures who are the primary breadwinners and defenders of the family and home. For many women, a man's ability to be a good provider and protector is considered the benchmark from which to measure a desirable partner. Yet, these same women will quickly add that qualities such as kindness and sensitivity are necessary to establish a lasting relationship in which communication between the partners flourishes.

The women also value a man who is faithful and honest and possesses a good sense of humor. Fidelity and honesty inspire trust while humor enables couples to celebrate life's joys and weather its disappointments.

I love big men with big hearts. A man who is whole and complete and emotionally sound. A man who generates a gentle warmth, possesses a calm nature and has inherited the wisdom of the ages. I love a man with a middle-aged face and an absolutely adult male body. A man whose strong hands reveal the truth about his sexuality. I love a big man with a deliberate grin, anticipating me.

— *Sanalli S. B. Phelps*
Hampton, Virginia

He embodies those qualities I love and cherish in my closest women friends, only clothed with his own distinct male energy. He is deeply sensitive, fearless, loving, selfless, tolerant, and compassionate. He truly likes and respects women, appreciating our differences, realizing we are two halves of the same endless circle. My mate would be spiritually centered and committed to doing all he can to enhance the world, his own life, and our relationship.

— *Denise B. McIver*
Los Angeles, California

He has passionate eyes filled with sunshine. What more can his heart reveal? He is all that is vulnerable, all that is tender, all that love could wish. He has a soul that shines with all its splendor. A faithful heart would not resist.

— *Edna M. Todd*
Los Angeles, California

Looking into his eyes, I see love, tenderness and warmth. When he smiles at me, the twinkle in his eyes makes my heart skip a beat, my knees go weak and butterflies flutter in my stomach. He is exuberant about life and finds pleasure in simple things. He generously shares of himself and his possessions. Sincere and honest, with a calming personality, he takes me places where I've never been.

—*Name Withheld*
Hallandale, Florida

He must not be afraid to show his vulnerabilities, because a woman that loves him won't exploit them.

—*Earline Jones Moore*
Dallas, Texas

My Mr. Right is a man who knows how to show his love. A man who always calls when you need to hear that calming voice... and makes you laugh. A man who would travel two hours by train and bus to visit. A man who would let you know when you are wrong and still makes you feel beautiful and special. A man who lets you know he feels blessed to have you.

—*Sherrill D. Scott*
Yonkers, New York

A Black man who is compassionate, communicative, and possesses a spiritual base that connects him to his divinity. He's devoted his life to the liberation of his people. He thinks before making decisions and doesn't choose violence as a release, yet is always prepared to defend his existence by any justifiable means. He has an unshakable inner strength and is willing to assist Black women in taking responsibility for fulfilling our collective purposes.

———*Monica L. Johnson*
Reseda, California

A listener with an open mind
A thinker with an open heart
A provider/doer/together...
An interpreter, when each person is not understood
A man with life, with faith, with the Lord

———*Malinda L. Rose*
Pittsburgh, Pennsylvania

The ideal man is, basically, a "loving giver." Without selfishness there is love. I envision my father to have been such a man. Though I didn't know my father, my ideal man is the man who possesses this same quality that I see in myself and that I now see in my children.

——— *Shirley Holliday*
Brooklyn, New York

He's naturally high waking up each and every morning. Mr. Right should be willing to make an honest effort to keep the doors of communication open in order to share life's ups and downs. Drawing from the core of his soul, my king would most definitely desire to treat me like the queen of his world. A back rub and massage will do just fine for starters.

— *Dianne G. Rankin*
Capitol Heights, Maryland

He's a passive thinker and a righteous brother who fights for the empowerment of Black people. He is a gentle, fair and honest man. He is a sensitive husband, an understanding father, a giving son, and a supportive brother. He is led by ambition, inspired by creativity, and sustained by love.

— *Catina Allen Bacote*
Brooklyn, New York

The ideal man is my rock in a weary land. He is a strong-willed, God-fearing man. He works hard to make his dreams a reality. Shows compassion and love to inspire you. A sense of humor to wipe your tears away. A man who is on the same page, same paragraph and same sentence as you.

— *Roxanne Williams*
Chicago, Illinois

The ideal man is considerate and kind. He is regal, yet gentle. He sends flowers for no particular reason. He wants to please you and wants to be pleased in return. He's no wimp. He's willing to try something new and different. He's confident, not arrogant. He's trustworthy. He's cordial to your family, even if he hates their guts. But most of all, my ideal man is my friend.

—*Anna Reeves*
Columbia, South Carolina

He knows what it means to compromise. He is the man that still kisses your stretch-marked stomach after bearing his children. He is God-fearing, not ashamed to turn over complicated situations to a higher power.

—*Tiffany Michelle Banks*
Atlanta, Georgia

Love, faith and compassion are traits that live in his heart and mind at all times. Enhanced with a mature sense of humor, he has the passion to be a good person. He possesses a strong sense of self, a manner of self-assurance that fits like a second skin. Respect for himself and others is first, not second-nature to him.

—*Valerie Y. Meekins*
Alexandria, Virginia

My Mr. Right...

Holds me all night,
Listens to my thoughts and adds his insight.
Plays party games,
 Not mind ones.
Is politically and spiritually conscious
 But still knows how to have fun.
Earns an honest living
 At something he likes.
Slows his roll,
 So I can keep up on my bike.
Loves my dog but never dogged a female.
Practices commitment and refuses to bail.
Maybe growls but never bites.
That's my Mr. Right!

—*E. K. Daufin*
Montgomery, Alabama

He's not built like Denzel, Wesley, or Billie. Makes you laugh, when you're down so you don't take yourself too seriously. Helps you wash your hair Saturday nights. Drives you crazy with the sweater that has patches of brown. Calls you early in the morning to see if you slept right. A paperbound book instead of flowers is his idea of romantic expression. Silently taking your hand, gently confirming you're his choice for life. Quietly making that commitment confession.

—*Diane M. Crews*
Rockville, Maryland

Simple things make up my ideal man. He is not ashamed to say "I love you," nor is he uncomfortable expressing affection in front of the "boys." He is not afraid of the "C" word (commitment), and the "F" word (future). He makes me laugh and laughs with me. He understands that true intimacy begins in the living room and not the bedroom and that I am his equal partner in friendship and love.

— *Carla O'Brien & Fran Henry*
Brooklyn, New York

He has a sense of humor that melts the ice and leaves you warm all over.

—*June A. Holloway*
Philadelphia, Pennsylvania

I would describe the ideal man as one who is unconditionally patient. He makes a lady feel complete. Compassion and communication add flavor. He is willing not only to teach, but also to learn. Romantically, he is selfless. The ideal man is analogous to a good stock portfolio: diversified.

—*Marilyn S. Johnson-Henry*
Madison, Alabama

Want Ad
The Colored Tennessean Newspaper, July 18, 1866

Wanted—— Correspondence, with a view to matrimony, by a young lady of agreeable disposition and pleasing features. Would prefer a young man of temperate habits—Wealth no object.

Oh! Had we some bright isle of our own,
In a blue summer ocean far off and alone,
Where a leaf never dies in the still blooming bowers,
And the bee banquets on through a whole year of flowers;
Where simply to feel that we breathe, that we live
Is worth all the joys that life elsewhere can give

Miss M. C. C., Lock Box 94, Nashville, Tennessee.

What Defines The Perfect Man?

Really listen to me.
Do you hear me?
Do you really understand me?
Please trust me. I can't make up for your past.
But I can change your future.
Love me, passionately... unconditionally... .
Can you see my tears?
Ask me why I cry.
Be patient with me.
I love you.
Pray with me, and look into my heart and see yourself.
Hold my hand as we walk together.
Sacrifice for me, I would too.
Be honest with me, I won't leave you.
Pledge your life to me, because I just want to love you.

—*Alvina Miller*
St. Petersburg, Florida

Intelligent, sensitive and caring... this Black man of God.
Whose touch is tender... yet arms so strong.
With kisses so sweet and a smile that melts my heart,
He loves me... yes, despite all my faults... .
Ideally, he is my best friend and all mine.

— *Sherry Hubbard*
Washington, D.C.

The Man

The Physical Ranks Inferior.
It's The Mind And What Occupies
This Device That Swoons Me So.
What About Strength?
Not That Machismo Mechanism.
A Man That's Aware
Of His Surroundings.
In Tune With Politics And His Society
And Yet Remains Restless For Change.
Sensitive.
Yeah, That's The Man.
Intellectually Endowed.
To His Sisters He Bestows
The Utmost Respect.
Stands His Ground.
Deeply Rooted In The Sacramental.
Praises To Jah.

—*LaShae A. Ferguson*
Washington, D.C.

The door to a positive, loving, caring relationship must be opened and the relationship entered by an honest man who holds the key.

—*Valerie Diane Bolling*
Stamford, Connecticut

The ideal man listens and is not prone to lash out in anger or haste. He doesn't solve his problems through abuse and doesn't blame others for his mistakes, but accepts full responsibility for his actions. He has a genuine relationship with God, which governs the way he treats his family, wife, lover and everyone else around him.

— *Roset A. Hollis*
Newark, New Jersey

My ideal man is one who is emotionally, spiritually and physically available. Not just in the bedroom... but also in the kitchen, as he shakes and bakes soulful recipes for maintaining a lasting commitment. A man who honors his truth as he demonstrates respect, loyalty and love. In essence, he is his own man and thus my passionate best friend.

— *Jonita Jo Jo Gass*
Philadelphia, Pennsylvania

Next to God, he is my rock. He is willing to experience and expand the nurturing aspects of his personality. He is a loving and gentle father. This man is thoughtful. He remembers birthdays and anniversaries. And he shares his innermost thoughts, yet he is a non-judgmental listener. We laugh together, play together, we are lovers. He is my best friend.

— *Phyllis Fuller*
Madison, Wisconsin

Whisper Words Of Love To Me

Tell me of thy heart's devotion,
When the sun has gone to sleep,
While the moon-beams kiss the ocean
And the stars their vigils keep.

Whisper softly, whisper gently,
Sweetest words of love to me;
Whisper so my heart can hear it,
All thy tenderness for me.

In the sunlight or the shadow,
On the mount or in the vale,
Tell me in the wood or meadow,
That thy love can never fail.

Tell me, though life brings its changes
Winter, summer, spring or fall
That it ne'er thy heart estranges,
That thy love will brave it all.

Lizelia Augusta Jenkins Moorer
1907

The ideal man, whom I have yet to meet
Would be a gentle man with compassion,
That knows how to be discreet.
He'd be self-assured, in no way arrogant,
With an honest, loving heart, possessing substance.
A man who regards women as his equal,
Put on earth by God above
To love, respect, and never neglect.
A hardworking, spiritual man,
Lacking nothing that properly belongs to him.

— *Robin A. Barlow*
New Orleans, Louisiana

Mr. Right Is A Man Who...

... has a sense of life's adventures.
... can laugh at himself.
... wants to be a good human being.
... is generous, not with his money, but with himself.
... has faith and pride in me.
... has the strength to love and be loved.
... appreciates what I can bring to his life.
... lets me be me.

— *Grace Salmon*
Toronto, Ontario

The ideal man's heart is open to everyone, but there's a special part only for his woman. His mind is sharp, and he has the good sense to acquiesce to the dictation of his heart. His heart instructs him to protect and provide for his family, look out for his friends, and be kind to strangers. His mind provides the book sense and street smarts to do so. Forget the physical, the ideal man is beautiful inside, where it counts.

—*Brenda Ann Griffin*
East Point, Georgia

Applauds my accomplishments and inspires me to greater ones. Doesn't need sex to communicate love. Knows listening is *never* optional. He makes me grateful for everyday I live to love him.

— *Samantha Hunter*
Mount Vernon, New York

When my day has gone downhill, he's willing to find a way to lift me up (even if he's had a messed up day himself). Since I have an illness, it would be comforting to know that someone will be coming home to me (even amidst all my pain), with a big ol' hug mixed in with an, "I love ya, my lady, and I will remain as equally committed as you to making this a 'fruitful' relationship!"

—*Kristi Camille White*
Alexandria, Virginia

He is not ideal this
ideal man
Perfection escapes his consciousness
Yet he is aware of his good side
ying and yang
light and dark
Spirituality does not
have him in church
every Sunday
Has him thinkin'
deep thoughts
about himself and the world
he lives in
Doesn't have to be Superman
to his Superwoman
Just needs to listen to
try to understand
beyond superficiality
He's the ideal man
Not so ideal
but beautifully
human and humane
yeah

—*Antoinette E. Clyde*
Amityville, New York

Three

Reveling In Her Strength

Respects Women | Respects Mother | Not Controlling
Not Intimidated By Her Strength, Success or Intelligence

No wavering here. A good man should appreciate the strength and resilience of Black women. He should be thankful for their roles as the bearers and nurturers of human life. He should cherish his mother for bringing him into this world and guiding his passage to manhood. A man's failure to follow any one of these basic principles will quickly eliminate him from the ranks of those who show promise of being ideal men.

Must this man sprinkle rose petals and spread lace before his adored lady's every step? Not at all. The women who speak in the following pages envision a man who knows that respect does not imply weakness and that gratitude does not mean servitude.

An ideal man merely gives a Black woman her due. The legacy of his foremothers demands it. The contributions of his sisters, tireless defenders of the home, nurturers of his children, and co-wage earners, cry out for it.

One who yearns to give a woman the respect she deserves and is worthy of. One who recognizes that making love starts before the bedroom. One who brings joy on those days when it seems the world is against you. One who knows that anything done without acknowledging the creator is without true substance.

—*Elaine M. Anderson*
Detroit, Michigan

Loves his mother and fears my brothers. Never tries to control or change me. He must respect me, and be willing to defend my honor.

—*Joilaina Diane Walters*
Cocoa, Florida

When I was a young girl, my ideal man was tall, dark and handsome. The kind of man who would make me lose my breath. With time, the picture has changed. He no longer has any specific physique. He's God-fearing and he respects his mother. He encourages me to have my own thoughts. He's not afraid to let me see him cry.

Did I lower my standards? No, not at all. I became a woman.

—*Esther M. Fitzgerald*
Kansas City, Missouri

23

The ideal man should definitely be a worshiper of the feminine spirit. He should celebrate his lady's spiritual and mental growth, not allowing chauvinistic ideas to cloud his expectations of what she can accomplish.

—*Debra C. McKnight*
Washington, D.C.

He would not be afraid of my independence; instead, he would embrace it, knowing that allowing me to be my own person would only enhance our relationship.

—*M. Coleman*
Indianapolis, Indiana

He is the person with *respect*. Respect for my womanhood, motherhood and his livelihood. He can understand the changes I go through (womanhood). When he also accepts the challenges my children will take me through (motherhood) and then live his life, be in mine and my children's, he's an ideal man.

—*Karen Session*
Inkster, Michigan

My Ideal Is Real

He isn't perfect, he's a real man; barber or doctor, he struggles to keep his head up. Even when discouraged, he talks to you and listens to you. He's unafraid of your strength, he bathes in it to renew his faith in himself. He gains faith from your belief in him and gives you the honor of loving him and being loved by him. He is a trying man, a real man, an ideal man.

—Maria Lourdes Gomez
Houston, Texas

Very spiritual. Knows God and where he stands in the scheme of things. Has a future. Fresh breath and clean teeth. Understands love is not a four-letter word and sex is a privilege, not a right. Understands that the Black woman is an asset, not a liability. The mother. Yemaya.

Understands he is precious with concern, not conceit.

Knows how to wash clothes and *does it*. Knows how to cook and *does it*.

And most of all, he should care. Please, just give a damn.

—Melissa L. Rawlins
Jamaica Queens, New York

Nwanyibuife

Nwanyibuife	*Woman is Something*
Gini bu ife?	*What is Something?*
Ife bu Ala	*Something is Earth*
Ife bu Mmiri	*Something is Water*
Ife bu Ekwu	*Something is Hearth*
Ife bu Nri	*Something is Nourishment*
Ife bu Udo	*Something is Peace*
Ife bu Nkwado	*Something is Support*
Ife bu Nkwudo	*Something is Wealth*
Ife bu Oganihu	*Something is Progress*
Ife bu Omumu	*Something is Reproduction*
Ife bu Ozuzu	*Something is Completion*
Ife bu Nne	*Something is Mother*
Gini bu Nne?	*What is Mother?*
Nne bu ndu	*Mother is Life*
Nne bu Ozuzu	*Mother is Rearing*
Nne bu Nchedo	*Mother is Protection*
Nne bu Ihunanya	*Mother is Love*
Nne bu Chi	*Mother is Chi*
Nne Ka!	*MOTHER IS SUPREME!*

Igbo (Nigeria) Song

The ideal man to me is someone who treats you as he would treat his mother. First of all, he should never hit a woman, yell or cuss at her. He should give her attention and show his feelings for her. He should also have goals the two of them can work together to accomplish.

—*Angela Stewart*
Alpharetta, Georgia

After an evening out, he doesn't drive to a hotel expecting something in return. He is in touch with his feelings and sure of his manliness. If the attraction is strong, he knows it's just a matter of time before she says "your place or mine?"

—*Wilhelmenia K. Boone*
Philadelphia, Pennsylvania

An ideal man would know how to treat, respect and admire his mother— the woman who brought him into this world. If a man doesn't know how to treat his mother, he will not know how to treat his woman.

—*Brenda Werdebach*
Warner Robins, Georgia

He respects me as a person, isn't controlling and doesn't treat me as his property. He gives me mind orgasms, and my body follows.

—*Pamela Modisette*
Gary, Indiana

He is not intimidated by a woman who knows what she wants in life.

—*Karen Gervais-Duzant*
Providence, Rhode Island

He's a warrior and will not be treated as a slave. He's not frightened by my step nor my stride and has embellished the throne for his queen to sit by his side.

—*Antionette Thompson*
Cleveland, Ohio

The ideal man is the man who treats his mom like a Queen, yet stands strong on his own beliefs.

—*Rochelle Beggs*
Brooklyn, New York

For this, their promise, and for their hard past, I honor the women of my race. Their beauty— their dark and mysterious beauty of midnight eyes, crumpled hair, and soft, full-featured faces— is perhaps more to me than to you, because I was born to its warm and subtle spell; but their worth is yours as well as mine. No other women on earth could have emerged from the hell of force and temptation which once engulfed and still surrounds black women in America with half the modesty and womanliness that they retain. I have always felt like bowing myself before them in all abasement, searching to bring some tribute to these long-suffering victims, these burdened sisters of mine, whom the world, the wise, white world, loves to affront and ridicule and wantonly to insult. I have known the women of many lands and nations— I have known and seen and lived beside them, but none have I known more sweetly feminine, more unswervingly loyal, more desperately earnest, and more instinctively pure in body and in soul than the daughters of my black mothers. This, then— a little thing— to their memory and inspiration.

W.E.B. DuBois
1915

Someone who isn't intimidated by my strength and independence but who embraces and encourages it. A companion, not a father. A lover, not a brother. A friend, not a critic.

——*Joan Finley*
Hillside, Illinois

He doesn't confine me to a box
He loves me for me, and I'm free to be me
He's a strong, loving and involved father, and the words
"I love you son" are commonplace
He's a risk taker, yet a realist
He's straightforward, honest, and sensitive
He's independent, yet he's not afraid to ask for help
But above all, he loves, respects, and fears God, and
He knows from where all his blessings flow.

——*Cathy H. Ways*
Lagrange, Georgia

He must possess a certain level of intellect in order not to be intimidated by me. He must not live beyond his means.

——*Wendy Taylor*
Valley Stream, New York

... *Last but not* least, he would have to be devoted to his mother. Because more than likely, the way he treats his mother is the way he'll treat you!

—*Pamela C. Parrish*
Indianapolis, Indiana

First, the ideal man would have a place for God in his life. Second, the ideal man would respect women and treat his woman like a Queen. She would treat him like a King. The ideal man would not have a problem with communication, trust, compromise and fidelity.

The ideal man would know that together, he and his partner could conquer the world!

—*Trina S. Hayes*
Columbus, Ohio

He must be my financial equal, bring knowledge and respect to our relationship, fulfill my needs and accept my strengths without feeling threatened.

—*Marcia K. Robinson*
Whittier, California

Must earn respect by the way he speaks and acts. Respect will be his if he shows himself to be steady, strong, and able to make decisions.

He listens to his wife's opinion, gives it consideration. Good provider— a must. Will have to understand the psychological differences between the two mates. Another vital factor— he won't forget her natural desire to feel needed.

Expressions of endearment are very important; a look, a touch, a word will go a long way for a woman.

—*Annie Jean Slade*
Milwaukee, Wisconsin

Four

Husbands, Fathers, and Brothers
Good Husbands | Responsible Fathers | Triumphant Brothers

A father who takes odd jobs removing garbage, selling scrap iron and blacktopping driveways to support his wife and eight children. A husband who gets a second job in order to buy a headstone for the graves of his wife's deceased parents, whom he never knew. A boyfriend who has fought drug addiction and becomes a responsible husband and father.

These are our men. They are around us everyday. We know them. They touch our lives with their strength, their laughter, and their dreams of a better tomorrow.

The triumphs of these men are certainly not what's reported in the news. Black men struggling to support those they love do not titillate audiences as do the negative images we are bombarded with on the evening news. Good copy these men may never be, but responsible fathers, good husbands, triumphant brothers, wonderful lovers, and yes, promising sons, they will always remain.

The passages by the women in the following pages proclaim their enduring love for our sons, brothers and fathers. These men were there in the past, they are there now, and they will be there forever— in body or in spirit.

My ideal man is my friend. Imperfect. He's someone you meet and exchange numbers for hanging out. No intentions of romance. Just chill. Most days you kick it; no make-up, just jeans and a ponytail. When the occasion calls for it, you dress up. You share past experiences, feelings and goals. You recognize talents, congratulate successes, and lend a shoulder when needed.

Morals intact. Spiritually grounded. Strong character. You watch out for one another, yet are cautious enough to let the other grow. Flaws are present. Nasty habits pluck your nerves. And then you realize, without any reservations, he's the one.

—*Jashondi A. Bibbins*
Virginia Beach, Virginia

He puts you, your needs and wants before his own. He's the one who has loved you from day one and continues to love you, in spite of. One who, while on lunch, fed your invalid mom in a nursing home and visited her every evening after work, before she died. One who plans, when the time comes, to care for your aging father and handicapped sister in our home, where they've lived for nine years.

—*Wanda Darling-Lee*
Beaumont, Texas

My father is the ideal man. Nothing but unconditional love and understanding. He has put up with his family for more than 45 years, through all happiness and sadness— even unmentionable horrors. Never complains. Always willing to help. Will go out of his way for each and every one of us. He can be called in the middle of the night out of the deepest sleep, the sweetest dream, and he will be there to help, with no questions asked. What more can you ask of a man?

—Paula G. Rose
Brooklyn, New York

When I am looking at that someone special and tears come to my eyes because he makes me happy. Waking up in the mornings or just rolling over and he is there, smiling and I just say "Thank you Jesus." Knowing when I say something it's heard (never having to repeat things over and over again). Accepting me for who I am and teaching me patience.

Safe and sound in my home he has created for us. I am married to Mr. Right!

—Carolyn Kanhan
Inglewood, California

I started to write down my opinion of the ideal man, but why do that when I am married to one? When I come home from my evening job, he has my warm bath and warm dinner ready. We talk about anything and everything, with him attentively listening to me. He is warm, passionate, affectionate, and supports my endeavors.

A lot of people turn their noses and heads at my city sanitation worker, but I love every inch of his body. This man goes above and beyond the call of duty to help others. That is why I admire, respect, honor, and love this hard-working man, who will always be my ideal man.

—*Monique C. King-Fuller*
Yeadon, Pennsylvania

When I am alone, thoughts of Avery make me smile and his presence makes me melt. His spirituality is his strength and his embrace is my comfort. He dreams impossible dreams and his determination makes them come true. He encourages me to be all of who I am, while giving all of who he is.

Before I close my eyes to sleep, I thank God for making a man who makes me complete.

—*Name Withheld*
Tulsa, Oklahoma

When I met him, he was working two jobs, going to school, and raising three daughters by himself. Now he works, cooks, cleans, and plays a major role in taking care of our six children. He spoils me every day of the week. He gives and does everything in his power for me. Now, I ask you, how much more ideal can you get?

—*Rosiland S. Tyler*
Ft. Carson, Colorado

When You Don't Stray From A Good Thing

He's the man occupying your dreams. You're sleeping with a big smile on your face only to wake up to find out you did, in fact, marry the man of your dreams.

—*Marjorie K. Murrell*
Warrensburg, Missouri

I walk into my house, again satisfied at the sight of a neat home, devoid of the mess I had made. Reclining on the sofa, with my sons on his lap, reading them a story, is my dream fellow. He is of medium height, slightly overweight, depicting a self-assurance independent of physical good looks. He flashes a smile as I enter the room, our eyes lock, our hearts touch, words are needless to express our sentiments.

—*Elsa Martinez*
Bronx, New York

My ideal man is not a husband, a lover, an ex-mate or a boyfriend. He is the father that I never had. He would be concerned about the welfare of his family and community. He would see my first steps and smile the first time he hears the word "Dada."

My father would see my achievements and accomplishments as I grow up to become a strong, Black woman like my mother whom he deserted before I was even born.

Even though this is all in my mind, such a man would be both my father and my ideal man.

> —*Tasha Huddleston*
> *Hopewell, Virginia*

Does the ideal man really exist? Yes, he does. He is the proud father of one adorable little boy whose birth transformed him into the man he is today— loving, focused, compassionate, self-assured and, most importantly, responsible.

I applaud this young man because society does not recognize young Black men like him— my brother.

> —*Vatel A. Jackson*
> *Alorton, Illinois*

The Union of Two
For Ife and Jacob Carruthers

what matters is the renewing and long running kinship
seeking common mission, willing work, memory,
melody, song.

marriage is an art,
created by the serious, enjoyed by the mature,
watered with morning and evening promises.

those who grow into love
remain anchored
like egyptian architecture and seasonal flowers.

it is african that woman and man join in smile, tears,
future.
it is traditional that men and women share
expectations, celebrations, struggles.
it is legend that the nations start in the family.
it is afrikan that our circle expands.
it is wise that we believe in tomorrows, children, quality.
it is written that our vision will equal the promise.

so that your nation will live and tell your stories accurately.
you must be endless in your loving touch of each other.
your unification is the message,
continuance the answer.

Haki R. Madhubuti

The ideal man would be the one I'm married to. After all, living with a woman tends to make a man more sensitive. He's not afraid to show his feminine side. He's self-assured and can still smile after working twelve-hour days, six days a week.

His thoughts are only of me. Did I eat okay? Did I take my vitamins? Did I get enough rest? He's spiritual and knows that there is a greater being than us. Last but not least, he is very caring; he even shovels the elderly's driveway as well as our own. He's my idea of a perfect man. Well, pretty close to perfect. Yes, I am an admirer of my husband.

—*Bernice Williams*
Euclid, Ohio

A Tribute To Avery From His Widow

He appreciates physical beauty, but he gets into his woman's head because he knows the real person is within. He makes love to her body and her mind, which in turn soothes her soul. He has a personal connection with God, giving him power and strength. He's focused and knows his purpose. He's strong yet gentle, playful yet sincere, a protector and friend. An ideal man's love will last even after his death.

—*Karen D. Day*
East St. Louis, Illinois

He is endowed with a dauntless strength of character and high moral standards. Though pierced by life's arrow, he refuses to surrender. He's a community leader who doesn't define his worth by mere assets.

Many times Black women complain that Black men are jealous of successful, strong females. This is not the case with Joseph. He actually encourages me to soar!

Spiritually, he relies more on networking with his God rather than networking with business associates. He cherishes his partner, loves his children, is romantic and enjoys laughter.

He considers me an equal partner, while understanding and accepting his role as the head of the family. He is politically savvy but does not hide his strong religious beliefs.

Talented? Yes! But humbled by praise. He's intelligent! He's awesome!! He's my husband!!!

—*Veronica D. Winston*
Lacey's Springs, Alabama

An ideal man is the figment of one's imagination. What's the next best thing? My husband.

> He loves me; I know it.
> He loves our children; they know it.
> His family comes first; we know it.
> We love him; he knows it.
> Bottom line.

Ideal man? Depends on the woman.

—*Julie T. Harris*
A   Ohio

My husband is my ideal   We were newly married, and I had a child of my own e   g into the marriage. It can be very difficult living in a step-family arrangement, but my husband handled the situation with love and patience.

After being married only two months, I unexpectedly became pregnant. When I married my husband I was a size 9, but by delivery I was a size 26. My husband made me genuinely feel as though I was the most beautiful woman on earth. He didn't love what I looked like but he loved who I was inside. Because of complications during the later months, we couldn't engage in sexual relations. My husband was very understanding during this time. He cared about my health and that of our unborn child more than temporary physical gratification.

Several days after I had the baby I became very sick. I had to stay in the hospital for three weeks. The first week, I was critical, so my husband stayed in the hospital with me day and night. He slept in a chair in my room and watched over and prayed for me like my guardian angel. We made it through that crisis and now have grown closer emotionally and spiritually... .

I'm back in school for my nursing degree. My husband supports the family totally because I stepped down from my full-time job making $25,000 - $28,000 plus benefits to pursue my degree. My husband works 12-hour days, picks up our children, ages 2 and 5, feeds, plays, bathes, and reads with them. He also does the grocery shopping, laundry and cleans the house when I have to study and go on my clinicals since this is my last year.

How can you describe the ideal man in such few words? My husband is patient, giving, nurturing, unselfish, an excellent father, lover, and friend. Most of all he allows me to be all that I can be, and all that I want to be. He is very supportive and encouraging. I love this man because he really loves me the way I want and need to be loved. I have my ideal man, my husband.

—*Jamentha Gaffney*
Cleveland, Ohio

My Ideal Man:

- is strong, funny, sexy and intelligent— all rolled into one.

- is not afraid to tell me how he feels about me in front of his single male friends.

- can sit with me on the sofa, with company present, and massage my feet after a hard day's work and not feel embarrassed.

- is not possessive, because he's secure with his manhood.

- has a job! He doesn't expect or need a woman or anyone else to take care of him.

- knows he's got it goin' on, and doesn't have to say it or repeat it over and over again.

- tells me he loves me before he leaves, and calls me ten minutes later to tell me again just in case I didn't hear him the first time.

He is my husband of two years, Treba Henderson. He is and does all the above and more.

—*Tina Exum-Henderson*
Fontana, California

The Woman Who Tamed Her Husband

Long ago, there lived a woman who was greatly saddened by her husband. The woman was sure that her husband no longer loved her. He never seemed to have time for her. He did not seem to care whether she was happy or sad or whether she spoke to him or not.

Distressed by this state of affairs, the woman consulted a local traditional doctor skilled at mending affairs of the heart. The doctor, after listening sympathetically to the woman's sorrowful tale, told her that he could help her to rekindle her husband's love. "But first" he told her, "Before I help you, you must bring me three hairs from the mane of a living lion."

Having tried, to no avail, everything she could think of to make her husband fall in love with her again, the woman was willing to undertake the dangerous task of plucking 3 hairs from a living lion's head. After considerable thought she came up with a plan to obtain the three hairs that the doctor requested.

The woman knew of a lion in the area that rested in the same spot not far from her village each morning. She decided that each day she would arise early and go to this spot and take the lion a young, healthy, plump lamb. And so, every morning she set out with a young lamb for the lion. With a prayer of thanks to the lamb, the woman would leave the lamb with the lion to meet its unfortunate fate.

As the days passed, the lion began to wag its tail when it saw the woman. Soon after, it even allowed her to stroke its head and touch its back. Finally, one day after much patience, the woman carefully plucked out three hairs while she was stroking the lion's mane.

The woman speedily delivered the three hairs to the doctor expecting to receive in return some sort of love potion. The doctor, pleased to see that she had obtained the three hairs, congratulated the woman and told her: "Now you are ready. Just as you have tamed the lion, go now and tame your husband."

Ethiopian tale

He could be your boyfriend, father, or in my case, my brother who taught me about family love and the love of life when he gave his life in an attempt to save another. He is my inspiration!

—*Jenelle Benoit*
Los Angeles, California

My father is my ideal man. He succeeded in taking care of his family despite the difficulties. He made sure his family had a place to live, food to eat and clothes to wear, and he showed his family lots of love. Quality time was very important to him. He would take us ice-skating, on family walks, and to the park. My ideal man helped me become the mother I am today.

—*Virginia C. Sherrod*
Richmond, Virginia

Mr. Right is my best friend. A person I can confide in and most of all, someone I can entrust with my life. I know he will always take good care of me. Well, my Mr. Right is my husband, Ken, of ten wonderful years! We share a beautiful seven-year-old son, whom we love and adore. With so much love in one home, what more could a person ask for?

—*Marcella M. Seay*
Auburn Hills, Michigan

Mr. Wright is my Mr. Right. He is my husband, lover, counselor, and advisor. He supports me 200% in whatever I do. While in school, he came home, cooked, helped the kids with homework, and continues likewise to this day. Every Sunday, he brings me breakfast in bed.

Recently, he worked two jobs to purchase a headstone for my parents' graves because I couldn't afford one earlier.

— *Sandra McAney Wright*
Palmetto, Georgia

Contrary to popular opinion, the ideal man is not necessarily tall, dark, handsome, and loaded with money. He could be only 5' 5" tall, yet still undeniably handsome.

He shares his life, is always in my corner, and is both my best friend and an ideal lover. He encourages and motivates me to be the best person I can be by being supportive of all my endeavors.

Yes, the ideal man is the man in my life.

— *Berthenia Rose Jackson*
Natchez, Mississippi

To describe the ideal man I should tell you about my husband, Robin. The adjectives that come to mind are faithful, charming, compassionate, understanding and loving. The way he treats me is with the utmost respect and admiration. He doesn't have the most money in the world or the best looks, but he loves me and that's all that matters.

— *Sonya M. Tarton*
Memphis, Tennessee

The ideal man is an intellectual with common sense. He is strong even when no one is looking. His beauty lies in his generous spirit and belief in God. He is nobody's victim and feels no need to carry his legacy like a cross. The ideal man loves his family and uplifts his community. My father and husband are ideal men.

—*Adrienne Maynard-Melchor*
Duluth, Georgia

Before I begin describing the ideal man, I would like to add that I have met many men from the East Coast to the West Coast, and the reason that I wanted to write this was that I wanted my husband and the rest of the world to know how truly special this man is to me and my family, and how I had always wondered if I would ever have that ideal man in my life. My husband was an only child, his mother died when he was small, his grandmother raised him, then he joined the Marine Corps and has become one of their exemplary senior enlisted personnel. I admire and respect the person that he is today. He gives selflessly and endlessly.

One would think, with such a tragic past, how can this be? He and my father share a similar background, and I love my father very deeply. I only hope that my husband's wonderful accomplishments won't go unnoticed. I'm sure that his mother would be just as proud of him as I am.

My ideal man:

> Is my friend
> Shares
> Loves my very being
> Doesn't care about my imperfections
> Is there by my side
> Doesn't talk, he shows me
> Makes special moments with care
> Stands tall when there are burdens to bear
> Is one I love and adore

> —*Vivian B. Mitchell*
> *29 Palms, California*

I am 38 years old and have been happily married for almost two years. This is the first time I have considered entering a contest of this nature. By no stretch of the imagination am I considered a writer, but your notice in *Essence* magazine has inspired me to write the following words:

Some would argue that there is no ideal man, but take it from me there is! He is strong, independent and totally self-sufficient. The man is confident and secure enough to acknowledge his need for nurturing and support. The ideal man is experienced in the ways of the world, yet innocent and pure of heart; willing to be loved and loves in return. Yes, God has blessed me with the ideal man.

— *Monice Williams-Alcendor*
Chicago, Illinois

The man of my dreams is the man I can love— not for what he can give me or do for me, but for how he makes me feel. One whose intelligence and integrity stimulate my mind. The man with the voice of an angel and a touch which awakens my spirit. His name is Antonio and when I look into his eyes, the beauty of his soul simply takes my breath away!

— *Belinda McGrew*
Phoenix, Arizona

He possesses my father's characteristics: honest, straightforward, kind, God-fearing, and most of all, part hustler!

When I was growing up, we were poor. Even though our food was rationed out at times, we never went to bed hungry. Dad supported his wife and eight children by working full time dumping rich people's garbage, selling scrap iron and black-topping driveways.

He did what it took for us to survive.

—*Carin D. Bradbury*
Cincinnati, Ohio

He continues to be your friend even though he wanted more from the relationship. He is there to help you pick up the pieces when things fall apart. This man takes the time to get to know you before he gets to *knnooww yoouu!*

He prefers to talk things over when you prefer to yell! He is intelligent, shy, and attentive to your every need. He's your homey, lover, friend. He is my fiancé, Wayne!

—*Tiffany Griffin*
Washington, D.C.

He is my best friend with whom I share all my deepest thoughts and desires. Our quality time spent together is priceless, which makes the difference in my life. He prays for me to keep me strong and to be everything that he needs. His love is never-ending, full and complete. He respects and protects me. He's not hard to find; he's my husband.

—Robin Baskerville–Swift
Carson, California

He is the man God has graced me with. His name is Michael Andrew Miller and he's 40 years old. He is the fifth child of six. He was born in Marshville, North Carolina. Michael was my next-door neighbor; we grew up together. His mother used to baby-sit me. She told me that when Michael was around six years old, he was watching a basketball game on TV and said he wanted to be a professional basketball player when he grew up.

Michael did become an all-American athlete while attending high school and proceeded to attend college to further his career in basketball. Unfortunately, Michael injured his right wrist in his sophomore year and was unable to fulfill his dream. He completed college with a bachelor's degree in psychology.

I have observed how this man's drive to better himself has helped him start at the bottom and continually work his way to the top. He is a man of God. We got married after dating for nine months. Michael took on a ready-made family of three—myself and two teenagers. Michael's drive to better himself has been his greatest asset. I have watched this man struggle with drugs and alcohol and look to God and a twelve-step program for help. He is musically inclined and he sings in our church choir. He plays the lead guitar, and helps out with our church basketball team. He volunteers and performs gospel shows for the Washington Home for the Aging.

Michael is currently a special education teacher, and he is enrolled in George Washington University's graduate program. He is a good father as well as a good husband. A strong Black man who continues to better himself by asking God first for daily direction.

—*Patty J. Miller*
District Heights, Maryland

As real and warm as sunlight, he is father, friend, brother, son, lover. A universal man. His mistakes are stepping stones. He is confident and accepts himself, embracing his sensitivity and his strength. He appreciates the sound of his lady's laughter and is able to lay his head on my breast when he just can't go any further. His arms are my security, his voice my joy. My ideal man is already mine.

—*Kirsten Morris*
St. Kitts, West Indies

<u>K</u>indness is his best quality.
<u>E</u>xtemporaneously creates delicious meals.
<u>I</u>nterested in serving mankind.
<u>T</u>houghtful gifts he presents often.
<u>H</u>andsome in and out of a Navy uniform.

<u>I</u>nspires me to follow my dreams.
<u>N</u>ever leaves the home without saying "I love you!"
<u>G</u>od orders his steps.
<u>R</u>ubs my feet when they are sore.
<u>A</u>ttention always given to his children.
<u>M</u>an oh man! I would marry my husband over and
over again!

—*Darlene Senicca Ingram*
Newport News, Virginia

Five

Rooted In The Spirit

Spiritual | Seeks God's Guidance | Knows He's Blessed

We are a people who gravitate towards the Spirit. In tune with God, in tune with nature. This observation accurately reflects the sentiments of the women in the following pages. For many women, a relationship is not limited to the interaction between a man and a woman. It must also embrace the couple's collective relationship with God.

According to the speakers in this chapter, an ideal man is, first and foremost, a Spiritual man. The strength of a Spiritual man is that he listens to, and is in continual dialogue with, the Creator. Because a Spiritual man is open to God's word, he seeks to live by His teachings and principles. Such a man will always turn to God when life's problems seem endless and answers are elusive.

A man's Spirituality directs his interaction with others and his expectations of himself— in ways more loving, more humane, and more responsible. It is not surprising then, that for most Black women, Spirituality is the key; one man, one woman, both with an affinity to their Creator.

Mr. Right puts God first in words, thoughts and deeds. Adherence to a disciplined spiritual life through daily prayer and meditation allows him to remain focused on the positive aspects of life. He gives the best of himself and receives the best from others. He lovingly embraces life and those around him to build up their confidence and self-worth.

— *Devra Garrett*
Milwaukee, Wisconsin

I believe God long ago chose my ideal man. Therefore, I have stopped trying to fix or fight what has already been worked out. I take the good with the bad, and wait patiently with all my heart through prayer and trust in Him. My ideal man will materialize, thus making him "the man" chosen to be my lover, my soul mate, my best friend... .

— *Nichol J. Galloway*
Capitol Heights, Maryland

A man who is wise at heart and strong-willed. Knows that God will supply all his needs. A man who is humble, charming and focused on God's word. A man that nurtures and loves his soul mate. Sharing his love with his children and community. He is the foundation of a Christian home.

— *Kimberly E. Telfare*
Daytona Beach, Florida

My ideal man is embodied in Christ. First, he has Moses' calling— he leads his family with conviction and vision. Second, he has Job's faith— the faith to see his family through the toughest circumstances. Third, he has Solomon's wisdom— wisdom to know in whom he should place his faith and trust. Lastly, he has Christ's compassion when Lazarus died— knowing that he's human and that a tear doesn't mean weakness.

—*Wilene Sanders Miller*
Slidell, Louisiana

My ideal man will get on his knees and pray by himself, or with his family to keep us strong and safe.

—*Minionette Rodgers-Jolly*
Atlanta, Georgia

How would I describe the ideal man? Well, first and foremost he must believe and know within himself that everything he has accomplished was done by God's will; and everything he wishes to accomplish can be done only through God who lives within him. He has a strong-willed ambition that creates an aura of success and makes others strong and positive simply because they are in his presence.

—*Rhonda Patrick*
Decatur, Georgia

And Now I Will Show You The Most Excellent Way

If I speak in the tongues of men and of angels, but have not love, I am only a resounding gong or a clanging cymbal.

If I have the gift of prophecy and can fathom all mysteries and all knowledge, and if I have a faith that can move mountains, but have not love, I am nothing.

If I give all that I possess to the poor and surrender my body to the flames, but have not love, I gain nothing.

First Corinthians 13: 1-3
The Holy Bible

First and foremost, he is spiritual. He has a true relationship with God. This man aspires not to break God's heart, therefore he'll try not to break yours. He lights up when the woman God has blessed him with enters a room. He sees great qualities in his woman and encourages her to pursue her goals. He leads his family in worship and prayer. His children look up to him as a role model instead of some athlete or Hollywood star. He loves unconditionally.

—*Jacquelyn Smith*
Swissvale, Pennsylvania

The ideal man is a born-again, Spirit-filled man of God. He loves me unconditionally because Christ loves him that way.

—*Rochelle C. Inglis*
East Lansing, Michigan

Acknowledges that he is subject to making mistakes. Looks towards a higher power to find balance, correction, love, compassion, and strength. Finds comfort and completeness in Him. Has faith that He is in control. Knows that he is truly loved. Above all, realizes that he can not help anyone until he seeks help for his own condition.

—*Bridgette Howard*
Aurora, Illinois

Simply put, he is a man who loves God and knows beyond a shadow of a doubt that God loves him. I believe that it is through God's love for us that we learn how to love ourselves and each other. A man who knows that God loves him no matter what, will find it easy to love his wife and his family unconditionally.

—*Dana L. Madsen*
Oakland, California

I now know that the right thing to look for in a man is faith. Whether it's God Almighty, Allah, or Jehovah, it doesn't matter. It matters that he believes that God is real and living in his life. It's a tough and cruel world out there and even Mr. Right has to call on Him from time to time.

—*Dorothy A. Cunningham*
Bronx, New York

He who loves God. Who understands that everyone is imperfect. That he is on a journey to correct himself, live life to its fullest, and that such a path pleases God. He accepts responsibility for himself, for what he is becoming, and what he does in this life. His journey is made easier with a helpmate, a friend at his side to help carry the load of living.

—*Alva Smith*
Thonotosassa, Florida

The Spiritual Basis Of Relationships

The seven principles of a relationship are: 1) physical 2) familial 3) temperamental 4) financial 5) emotional 6) cultural, and 7) Spiritual.

Spiritual compatibility is the capacity to look beyond the first six principles of a relationship to reveal the most enduring nature of a soul mate— the interaction of each partner with the Creator. In broad terms, Spirituality is the state of being concerned with the soul. Spirituality is separate and apart from the other relationship principles in that it has everything to do with inner collectiveness. It is the innate desire that one has to gravitate towards the Creator and live a compassionate life. Without a Spiritual component, a relationship is bound to fail.

With astronomical divorce rates, the breakdown in family structures, and the insatiable hunger for more consumer goods, we need to re-examine the basis for why people meet, what makes them stay together and which components make for a long-lasting, mature and life-giving relationship. We need to focus more on what works; not on what has failed time and time again.

Human beings are complex and to reduce relationships to a set of rules is futile. That is why we need to look at Spirituality as the foundation of a relationship between two human beings.

A Spiritual relationship is mutual and assumes that we are more than just beings who eat, sleep and breathe. It demands that we seek God in all his forms. Our Spiritual needs have to be fulfilled in order for us to fully become all we can be!

I have been married for 20 years and I am aware that our relationship is not primarily sexual, but it is Spiritual. However, what initially attracted us was physical, sensual, and sexual. I recognize that as time passes, the body will surely fail, financial security may become jeopardized with the loss of a job, a family member may become addicted to drugs or alcohol, and the children will grow up and leave (as I have experienced with my four children). But what will always remain is the Spirituality of soul mates.

The most connected I am to the woman I married is when we are at peace within ourselves... it is what I do, not what she does that makes the relationship grow. And what I do must involve matters of the soul.

The Very Rev. Petero A.N. Sabune

This man is intimately aware that there is a power greater than himself guiding all things. The fruits of this understanding and commitment to that greater power make it possible for him to embrace his brothers and sisters in the human family.

He is guided by humble confidence with truth, compassion, selflessness, strength, empathy, faith and hope. He is in control of his actions, yet he has an unwavering passion for life.

—*Afrika Afeni Mills*
Brighton, Massachusetts

The ideal man must not only be spiritual, but spiritually equipped to withstand the battles of this world. He must be bold enough to stand and say, "I love the Lord," and also, "I love my woman." His inner peace and joy must run deep enough to enable him to laugh and keep me laughing through my troubled times.

Also, he must be sensitive enough to know when I am having a time dealing with this world's struggles. He must be confident enough to allow me, his partner, the freedom to do "a day out" with friends or family.

—*Penny Denny*
East Spencer, North Carolina

A responsible African-American man, that loves, worships and praises the Lord. Attends church consistently, enjoys tithing. Working, with consistent income, and can help pay the bills. He's loving, caring, sensitive (to my needs). Enjoys family activities and communicating (with me). Likes to travel and tries new activities. Smiles, likes to laugh. Good personal hygiene. Knows how to be pleasing when intimate. Cleans up after himself.

— *Deborah G. Murphy*
Detroit, Michigan

Willing to compromise everything except his morals and values.

— *Lisa Truitt*
Baton Rouge, Louisiana

A few years back when I was young and impetuous, the ideal man for me would have been someone like Michael Jackson, Al Greene, the Indian from the Village People or any other rich, sexy, famous man with an expensive car. But, now that I'm older and a *little bit* wiser, the ideal man for me is an extremely unselfish, loving carpenter who heals the sick, answers prayers, performs miracles, saves souls and gives life everlasting.

— *Carylon Ann Jerry*
Americus, Georgia

I Know Moon-Rise

I know moon-rise, I know star-rise,
Lay dis body down.
I walk in de moonlight, I walk in de starlight,
To lay dis body down.
I'll walk in de graveyard, I'll walk through de graveyard,
To lay dis body down.
I'll lie in de grave and stretch out my arms,
Lay dis body down.
I go to de judgment in de evenin' of de day,
When I lay dis body down,
And my soul and your soul will meet in de day,
When I lay dis body down.

Negro Spiritual

———————

The ideal man to me is a vision conceived in the mind, believed in the heart and achieved through love. You can take the best a man has to offer and tear him down or his worst and make him better. A man who reaches inside himself to understand his purpose for being, searches out the creator (God) for the knowledge to understand himself, according to His perfect will and attains the wisdom necessary to execute the plan. Compassion, strength, intellect, maturity, kindness, gentleness, humility and a desire to live as God has already commissioned.

— *Susan Vermelle Wadley-Williams*
New Haven, Connecticut

Above all, he is a man who loves God. He acknowledges that through God, all things are possible if he just believes. He's strong enough to cry, but not weak enough to give up.

—*Bila Rometa Collins*
Memphis, Tennessee

My ideal man knows he is a spiritual being operating as God's vessel. He sees others as spiritual beings fulfilling a divine purpose. He loves unconditionally and shares his gifts unselfishly.

—*A. Shahnaaz Davidson*
Verona, Pennsylvania

When I first thought about the qualities I would like in my ideal man, physical attributes came to mind. Then I looked in the mirror and said, "Girl, you ain't all that yourself." Looking beyond the physical, my ideal man would believe in God and be deeply rooted in and by His words from Psalms 1: 3, "And he shall be like a tree planted by the rivers of water." Once he has that solid rock to stand on, the rest would be easy to build on.

— *Stephanie Renee Parker*
Memphis, Tennessee

Everyone has her own perspective on Mr. Right. But most of all, I would like for my Mr. Right to be spiritual because through the Creator, we are all Mr./Ms. Right.

—*Magellan Bradley*
Columbus, Ohio

Most importantly, Mr. Right is sent by divine order to fill an empty love space. My husband is all that and more. Thank God for showing me and our community that He truly does make Mr. Rights.

—*Valerie J. Code*
Jacksonville, Florida

In The Name Of Allah, The Beneficent, The Merciful

O people! Be careful of your duty to your Lord, Who created you from a single being and created its mate of the same kind and spread from these two, many men and women; and be careful of your duty to Allah, by whom you demand your rights, and to the ties of relationship, surely Allah ever watches over you.

Sura II, Sec. 1.
The Holy Koran

The Ten Commandments Of Ideal Manhood

You shall have no other Gods Before Me (Loyal)
You shall not worship any other Gods (Loyal)
You shall not take the Lord's name in vain (Sensible)
Remember the Sabbath Day (Responsible)
Honor your Father and Mother (Respectful)
You shall not murder (Forgiving)
You shall not commit adultery (Faithful)
You shall not steal (Generous)
You shall not lie (Honest)
You shall not covet your neighbor's house (Grateful)

— *Cindy Hamilton*
North Augusta, Georgia

He acknowledges that serving God is the most important part of his life. He can't respect any woman unless he respects himself and the God that lives inside him.

—*Jolaine Walker*
Flint, Michigan

He is a man of God and believes that through faith he can achieve abundance and peace in life. He understands his role as a provider.

— *Tiffany Ellzy*
Brooklyn, New York

Six

Making It Plain
Level-Headed Man | Real Father
A Scared-Of-Nothing Man | Erections In Check
Mr. "All Right For Me" | Keeping The Commitment
Kissing Toads Before The Prince

Exhausted by the trials of a demanding day, Nubia let her paperback slip from her fingers onto the cluttered bedroom floor. Wearily, she turned off her nightstand light and burrowed deeper into the tousled covers on her bed. As she tumbled more deeply into sleep, an enchanting ending to the novel she was reading danced across her mind. She was no longer a voyeur to the heroine's frenzied flight across the sunbleached desert to escape a band of villains. Now, unspoken dreams and unfulfilled desires tumbled forth. Nubia became the heroine caught up in the longing for her prince to save the day... .

Nubia stumbled as she struggled to walk across the hot desert sand. Suddenly, a richly adorned royal caravan majestically working its way across undulating desert slopes appeared on the horizon. An image of her prince sitting astride his powerful stal-

lion as it thundered across the distance to her rescue sent a thrill of warmth through her body.

Her breath was taken away when the prince vaulted from his stallion with practiced ease and rushed to her side, his magnificent cape billowing and swirling behind him. Effortlessly, he swung her up into his arms and embraced her surely against his powerful chest, pledging to love and cherish her for all eternity...

We don't think so!

As you read the following passages, you may be surprised to find that even when the speakers are whimsical and dreamy, their ideal men are not fairy-tale heroes. There are no dreams of richly adorned royal caravans travelling through the desert sand and certainly, no princes vaulting off their magnificent steeds to rescue their lady-loves from evil pursuers.

For *real* women, flesh-and-blood human beings with emotional, physical and material needs, the ideal man must be capable of dealing with the *real* world. Unfortunately, sensitive and communicative isn't going to cut it if the man doesn't have a j-o-b, is not diligently seeking one, or is not educating himself in preparation of one. No, the ideal man must meet some of those earthly requirements that our parents say we should look for in a man. These include having a job, being independent (i.e. not living in his mom's basement), being drug-free, being a real father to all his kids (not just a sperm donor), and keeping his erections in check.

Some of the women in the following pages are fortunate—they have found their *real* ideal men. Others, knowing what our men are capable of, remain hopeful. Hopeful of finding a man who is ideally suited to them. A man to help create something that is bigger and more beautiful than each in their own separate worlds.

I have heard a lot of women say to their friends, "Girl, if he ain't got no car, he can't do nothin' for me!" or "McDonalds? He can't afford me working at no McDonalds!" My theory: minimum wage is better than no wage. These days, if you find a man with a 9 - 2 job you're doing pretty good for yourself. At least you don't have to worry about those pages from T-Bone or dodge bullets every time you go out. I think these days, women have their standards set a little high. So what if he drives a '79 Pinto to Brookshires to bag groceries. Give the man some credit. He's trying. An ideal man shouldn't have to be just rich in the pockets. He should be rich in mind, spirit, intelligence, personality, etc. Shall I go on, my sistas?

—*Anitra Gardner*
Wilmar, Arkansas

Idealism is a concept that troubles many a union and dooms its longevity to ultimate disappointment. So instead of "the ideal man," I want "a deal man": a man who keeps up his end of the deal, whatever deal was made. Who lives up to his word, whatever his word may have been. Who treats me at least as well as he is treated by me. If you are he, let's make a deal.

—*Sharon Harris*
Norcross, Georgia

My ideal man is my best friend, has a "j-o-b" and files a W-2 yearly. He is spiritual, honest and has a dependable automobile. This ideal man handles anger without inflicting physical, verbal or mental abuse. He is a leader with a sound mind, a thoughtful soul, and a witty and charming personality. He has his favorite hobbies, but is willing to learn new ones. That's my man!

—*Katrina Lawrence-Martin*
Rome, Georgia

Not only a sperm donor but a real father.

—*Anissa P. Ben*
Prentiss, Mississippi

My ideal man would be one of great integrity and spiritual strength. He'd be compassionate, forgiving and have a great sense of humor. A man whose priorities would begin with his family and friends and extend to his own dedication to seek success and happiness.

Unfortunately, this is the real world. Time to toss out the complex description of Mr. Right and be thankful for a level-headed brother with a job!

—*Shelina Dawn Wallace*
Philadelphia, Pennsylvania

The ideal man will know how to handle going to bed one night next to a coke-bottle-figured woman and waking up to a woman with a milk-jug body. A woman's body goes through hell and if a man loves her, he will support her while her body goes through drastic changes until she resolves her weight problems.

Also, this man will know that if he has to hit, it's time to split. The only time he will raise his hands to her is to hug her, feed her, or rub his big hands all over her body. A real man will know how to cope with stress without taking it out on the lovely woman that is by his side.

The ideal man will give his woman love, love, and more love. The African-American woman needs to be praised and recognized by her man, for we have been manipulated, violated, and discriminated against since the beginning of time. We are back-breaking, hard-working, women that deserve to have our feet propped up by our men.

The African-American woman is just like Hagar in the Book of Genesis, true survivors.

—*Jacqueline Lenore Hollingsworth*
Dallas, Texas

*W*aiting To Exhale

To: Waiting to Exhale
From: Taking a Deep Breath
Re: The Ideal Man
cc: Any Man Who Needs A Clue

Hey Girl:

This one might be the one. I know it's only been a couple of months, but he still answers my pages within 10 minutes. It must be love. We took a walk in the rain last night. Kinda' reminded me of that last scene in *Love Jones*. You *know*, when the lovers get back together, but they're not sure how to work things out, but it's okay 'cause love will save the day. Um hm, girl. I even told my mother about this one, and you know that's serious.

I met this man two months ago today. He is 28 years old, gainfully employed, divorced, and has one child. It used to be that we would call him a first time loser. But today, I want a man who has tried this love thing already. By now, he knows what he wants and how to keep it. Experience, these days, is more important than energy (if you know what I mean).

Anyway, I truly enjoy spending time with him for a number of different reasons. I believe and have evidence that we connect on so many different levels (but, y'all don't hear me though). It is not often that I come into contact with anyone, male or female, that is my intellectual match— except you of course— that is not intimidated by someone else's intelligence. You *know*, smart ain't never been sexy where we come from. At the same time, he makes me laugh until my stomach hurts. He is sensitive and affectionate and no less masculine for it. There's just enough sugar in the Kool-Aid to make it sweet, but still smack your lips at the tartness.

He has goals and aspirations and actual plans to achieve them that he is actively pursuing. He is supportive and nurturing without trying to solve my problems or "fix" me. When I share my concerns with him, he listens quietly and doesn't volunteer a response unless I directly ask for his opinion. When I ask, only then does he give me a thoughtful reply that's tailored to my personality and the actual circumstances without giving me a short anecdote about a similar situation he has experienced.

And girl, he loves my child-bearing, baby-carrying-hips, sit-a-TV-on-it-butt, breast-giving-in-to-gravity body. In fact, he worships it. He is both a tender lover and a wild freak in bed. He is willing to experiment, ask questions, and not pass judgment on my prowess. He is also an excellent teacher. I've learned a great deal about the male anatomy and its pleasure points. But more importantly, I've even learned more about my own.

Let me stop now, 'cause I can write for another two hours and I don't have a change of underwear with me. Girl, just be happy for a sister, for now. I hope I won't be sending you a sob story next week. But for right now, I think I found that ideal man. Love ya' girl. I'm Audi. Peace.

—*Tara Hogan*
North Hollywood, California

I am looking for an all-grown-up, ain't-scared-of-nuthin',
and know-it's-time-to-save-the-race man.

Good-husband, good-lover, good-worker, good-warrior
kind of man.

A read-a-book, loves-black-women, protects-black-children
and never-hit-a-woman kind of man.

A turn-the-TV-off-and-let's-talk-or-make-love-instead
kind of man.

A spoil-me-rotten-kind-of-man.

—*Leonia Collins*
Marietta, Georgia

He appreciates the inside of a woman as well as the outside. Accepts things he cannot change and makes a real effort
to change the things he can, instead of running away. The
ideal man knows and realizes that his erections are not his
main source of manhood.

—*Sonia Watson*
Houston, Texas

Excerpt From "The Woman"

"They say" that men don't admire this type of woman [the independent woman], that they prefer the soft, dainty, whining, mindless creature who cuddles into men's arms, agrees to everything they say, and looks upon them as a race of gods turned loose upon this earth for the edification of womankind. Well, this may be so, but there is one thing positive... no matter how sensible a woman is on other questions, when she falls in love she is fool enough to believe her adored one a veritable Solomon. Cuddling? Well, she may preside over conventions, brandish her umbrella at board meetings, tramp the streets soliciting subscriptions, wield the blue pencil in an editorial sanctum, hammer a type-writer, smear her nose with ink from a galley full of pied type, lead infant ideas through the tortuous mazes of c-a-t and r-a-t, plead at the bar, or wield the scalpel in a dissecting room, yet when the right moment comes, she will sink as gracefully into his manly embrace, throw her arms as lovingly around his neck, and cuddle as warmly and sweetly to his bosom as her little sister who has done nothing else but think, dream, and practice for that hour. It comes natural, you see.

Alice Dunbar-Nelson
1895

Mr. Right for me has to be a BMW (Black Man Working) that is not down with OPP (Other People's P___) that has a positive TRW credit report and a negative HIV test. He has a healthy sense of humor, while not necessarily being a Bernie Mack in training. He visits his local library or bookstore on a regular basis, but *Revenge of the Nerds* is not his favorite movie.

He should have a healthy, down-to-earth sense of self without being the poster boy for the conceited. Spirituality is the key. He should have a higher source to turn to.

—*Antonia Facen*
Detroit, Michigan

The ideal man strives to meet his personal standards and those of the woman he loves— not those of a racist, macho society or his "boys." He is honest— no frontin' or playing Mr. Mack. He knows real women are interested in sharing in his love and life's journey, not his bank account.

In truth, every jewel has its flaw but a man who seeks peace and balance through a Higher Power is perfection regardless.

—*Jamilla B. Coleman*
Atlanta, Georgia

I don't know if the ideal man exists. Unfortunately, finding the ideal mate often becomes more of an ordeal. Perhaps finding the right person depends on us first becoming the right person. Of course 1 right man plus 1 right woman may not equal happiness. The key is to be right for each other. My divine Mr. Right is God-fearing, spiritual, strong, and somewhat handsome (but not prettier than me). He knows how to save money as well as spend it, and wants to raise a child rather than be one. He's not necessarily ideal; he's the real deal!!

—*Rachel R. Wilson*
Ft. Worth, Texas

One that is real and true. He deals with the good and the bad, especially if he decides to say "I do." Taking full responsibility, not just receiving the benefits of marriage. Being there for you in more ways than one and being a real daddy to his kids. Having a job. Being the man, not just your lover.

—*JoWanna Lynn Etheridge*
Birmingham, Alabama

Many women today define Mr. Right as a money man. In my opinion, the "Benjamins" are irrelevant. Mr. Right should be faithful and devoted. In truth, I don't think there is such a thing as Mr. Right until we become Miss Right.

—*Crystal J. Norris*
Eagle Lake, Texas

𝒯he Perfect Guy

Old-fashioned: One of the nearly extinct men who don't expect me to be responsible for their financial needs.

Ambitious: Not imprisoned by self-imposed racial restrictions.

Religious: Only the power of God can keep him from the snares of those oh so many single sistas.

Real: Accepts me as I am— in rollers and a net. Rollers at night create *my* morning crowns of glory.

Heterosexual: I have no desire to compete with "Bill" for his attention.

—*Chyrille P. McIntosh*
Miramar, Florida

𝓗e stands beside me, not over me
I love him for who he is and not for whom
    I want him to become
I am his lover, never his mother
We are best friends now and forever
I love him always and all ways
If ever two were one then certainly we
He may not be Mr. Perfect but he's Mr. Good
    Enough For Me.

—*Latonya L. Dilligard*
Winston Salem, North Carolina

Excerpt From "Anticipation"

... He was like men all over the world when they are stirred by feminine charm: a shapely leg, the flash of an eye, the quiver of a nostril, the timbre of a voice, and the male species becomes frenzy personified. Many men go through this sort of mania until they reach their dotage. The cynics among them treat women with a little flattery, bland tolerance, and take fine care not to become seriously entangled for life. Women, on the other hand, use quite a lot of common sense: they are not particularly thrilled by the physical charms of a man; if his pockets are heavy and his income sure, he is a good matrimonial risk. But there is evolving a new type of hardheaded modern woman who insists on the perfect lover as well as an income and other necessaries, or stays forever (away) from the unbliss of marriage.

Mabel Dove-Danquah

Mr. Right does not exist! With that out of the way, I can describe my idea of a decent man. His name is All Right For Me or ARFM for short. He has a wonderful smile, with a great set of clean white teeth and pleasant breath. He isn't a liar or a sneak; he's honest 90% of the time.

ARFM is generous, he isn't cheap with his feelings or his money. I wouldn't have to constantly wonder about how he feels about me or pay for our dates. He communicates well with his vocal cords instead of his fists.

ARFM makes me laugh more often than he makes me cry. He isn't ignorant. A college degree would be nice but isn't required; a high school diploma is.

Mr. ARFM isn't the sexiest; he can cook better than I can and wouldn't mind ironing my blouses once in a while. He doesn't pressure me for sex or anything that I'm not comfortable with. He doesn't degrade women. He celebrates them for their mystery and beauty. ARFM isn't conceited or arrogant. He believes in and practices safe sex.

Last but definitely not least, he has to have a job. I don't really care whether he is a messenger on a moped or an attorney with a Mercedes.

— *Stacy R. Williams*
Brooklyn, New York

Unfortunately, I have almost resorted to buying a genie lamp! I tell my friends, "Rub a lamp 'cause it ain't happening!" Even with that said, I truly have hopes for my ideal man.

He's honest, committed (not in an institution), respectful, a good listener, sensitive, aspiring, employed, and can accept someone with an illness (important).

Oh yes, good teeth, shoes and hairline! No need to spend quality time at the dentist's, Buster Brown's or buying hair plugs.

—*Jacqueline Andrews*
Brooklyn, New York

My ideal man does not have to be handsome but he must be drug-free. Flowers and romance are nice but I'm a practical person. I need a man to help me financially. I am not requesting his whole paycheck because I know he has bills of his own. I am asking for little simple things like buying groceries (for our enjoyment), performing regular maintenance on my house and car. I also need to know that he loves me when I am my weakest and ugliest; I do not want to be dignified all the time.

—*Lisa Yvette Brim*
Martinsville, Virginia

My past experience with men has made me wake up to a whole new beginning of what a relationship is all about. I want to feel real love and total intimacy. I don't want to be just a knickknack on the shelf or a trophy. I want to be much more than a collectible. My man has to make me feel needed when I'm with him, without my feeling like a pawn. Do men really listen with their ears or with their eyes? I have seen lots of women passed over because men want Barbie Dolls. We are not artificial. We are real. We unfortunate girls make really good mates. I want a spiritual man who believes in God, has a sense of direction in his life, wants to grow, and wants to take control of his life.

— *S. P.*
Camden, New Jersey

He says he likes you best in the morning with wild un-saloned hair— "You look so natural."

He spices your tea perfectly every time.

He believes PMS (Personality Mutation Syndrome) is a genetic disorder— you can't possibly be held accountable for your actions.

He says things like "Whatever you want, Honey," or "Baby, you don't need to lose a pound."

He's sexy educated, employed, spiritual, strong natured, reliable. He's...

— *Ki'Bora*
Kansas City, Missouri

I remember when I was in high school, I had an in-depth conversation with my best friend, Lori. Of course, the subject was boys and what our perfect guy would be like.

"Boy" would have Michael Jordan's height. The face and body of Stoney Jackson, athletic ability of Earl Brown (a boy on my street), a voice like any member of New Edition, and Kwame's hair. Of course, he would have to be as suave as big Daddy Kane. Our guy was perfect.

As I have grown older and wiser, at the age of 25, my description of this "boy" has drastically changed. My ideal man has become more grounded in his spirituality. He has set both short-term and long-term goals for himself and the love of his life. My ideal man appreciates that he comes from a small, rural town but is open-minded to his complex world. He has a strong sense of self and he questions authority.

My ideal man is honest about his feelings and will tell the world he is in love with me. He knows how to love and be loved in every sense of the word. He always asks me how my day was and he makes me laugh. My ideal man is Black and he is strong inside and out. He encourages me to excel and supports all my efforts. My ideal man loves and respects his mother and he can cook too! In essence, my ideal man is Brian Lamar Hobbs.

—*Jennifer L. Colter*
Bowie, Maryland

Seven

Creative Expressions
Words With Flavor | Words With Soul

In the following passages, women beautifully capture the best that a loving man has to offer a woman. Here, ordinary words have been turned into creative expressions of women's most cherished dreams and private thoughts. Whatever the many distinguishing characteristics in their descriptions, there is one clear common denominator; these women long for men who are willing to offer the best of themselves on every level—spiritually, emotionally, physically, mentally and sexually. They remind us that ultimately, the intangibles a man brings *to* a relationship are the measure of his value *in* a relationship.

He that loves with his whole heart, knowing the risks but taking the chances. He that broaches life with truth, faces failure with dignity, embraces love with commitment. He that loves with entirety, gives without reservation, and respects without limit. He that embraces struggle with endurance, sorrow with hope, and anger with the promise of forgiveness. When I have lost my inspiration, it's his face that inspires me. The ideal man: husband, lover, father, friend.

— *Cassandre Genevieve Harper*
Groton, Connecticut

Daydreaming, she smiles at his strongest features; a mother's nagging which masks endless pride; a sister who testifies to his gentle protectiveness; and friends who respect this man's mental strength. He brought her fresh white roses. She never had to plead for them. He only listened to their conversation. He will apologize, criticize, and sympathize. A glimpse at her face tells him whether he should try again, again, and again.

— *Name Withheld*
Sewickley, Pennsylvania

This man engages in relationships which embrace non- traditional gender roles. His ambition is guided by the omnipotent, ever-loving Jah. His passion for splendors of nature at its best is innate... creation of life, and honor.

— *Maureen Ghans*
Brooklyn, New York

Touch Me, Fool Me, Call Me On Monday
(Ideal Man For Any Woman)

Exhilarating, intoxicating
Stimulating, invigorating
Smooth-talking, cool-walking
More man than the average man
Large hands reaching out
Absorbing my hands in yours
Luscious lips swallowed mine
Mint taste left on my tongue
Biceps, triceps big as tree trunks
Wrapped around my arms
Chest as wide as the ocean
Pressed upon my breast
Small waist
My arms circle your belt
Long legs stretched as far as the river
Big feet like ships carrying tons
Irresistible, quite convincible
Touch me, fool me, but, call me on Monday

—*Linda Moses*
Raleigh, North Carolina

It is really quite simple. The ideal man is one who brings you joy. At every waking moment, there is a happiness that is easily explained and summed up in one word, a name, a person. At every sleeping moment, the subconscious is keenly aware of the rapture that lies within your soul. With every breath, there is love and with every sigh, there is comfort. The ideal man is satisfaction.

——*Lekeisa F. Rockwell*
Hutchins, Texas

I think the ideal man should be a man who is not afraid of criticism and can speak his mind. A man who knows that he is not perfect but strives to improve himself; who can be supportive of others even though he has not accomplished his own goals; who understands the difference between loving and being in love; who knows his limitations but loves the challenge. A simple man who loves himself and God.

——*Jacqueline B. Blake*
Denton, Maryland

It is not about height, looks or profession. It's about someone who should not change on your account, shares your whole life with you, and takes the good with the bad.

——*Name Withheld*
Seale, Alabama

*I*deal Man Étouffeé

4 cups honesty
4 cups commitment
2½ cups generosity
3 cups confidence
3 cups ambition
2 cups each of adventure, romance, and attentiveness
1 cup each of sensuality, compassion, sexiness, masculinity
and respect for women.

Stir in 2 tbsp personality, 1 tbsp each style and sense of humor, and a pinch of handsome to taste. Preheat oven to 350 degrees, bake to desired shade and stature. Serve with a sense of family and a side of gentleman.

0 grams fat
0 calories

——Rochelle K. Thomas & JaMonica Jackson
Houston, Texas

He has the wit of Bill Cosby, the courage of Nelson Mandela and he is Denzel Washington "fine," if only in my mind. We are quite the team and as imperfect people in an imperfect world, we are ideal.

——Tomie Jean Marshall
Detroit, Michigan

Love

While tracing thy visage, I sink in emotion,
For no other damsel so wond'rous I see:
Thy looks are so pleasing, thy charms so amazing,
I think of no other, my true love, but thee.

With heart-burning rapture I gaze on thy beauty,
And fly like a bird to the boughs of a tree:
Thy looks are so pleasing, thy charms so amazing,
I fancy no other, my true love, but thee...

George Moses Horton
1829

Wanted. God-fearing single Black male between the ages of 24 and 30, seeking a serious monogamous relationship. College education is a plus but established and successful businessmen may also apply. Must be strong-willed and ambitious by day while loving and understanding at night. A faithful soulmate always respecting and yearning for my opinion.

Those who entertain falsifiers need not apply. Taking pride in one's appearance is mandatory but applicant must not be conceited or vain.

—*Pamela Johnson*
Topeka, Kansas

The essence of my ideal man lies in his foundation, and his heart and soul. His building blocks should include God, family, a strong work ethic and a healthy sense of self. Whether he's got a blue collar, white collar, or no-collar job, he should be able to take care of his responsibilities.

Features and looks are nice but there is nothing like a fit or flabby pair of biceps wrapped around a sister in her darkest hour.

—*Altha Thompson*
Chicago, Illinois

The ideal man is an artist. Like a poet he is unrestrained. With his words his heart never lies and to himself he stays true. Like a dancer he reacts to the world around him, yet moves to his own beat. Like a sculptor, because his touch is like no other. When he touches your mind, heart and soul, he leaves a lasting impression. Just as a painter, no matter how dark it gets, he paints life in the most brilliant colors.

——*Tiffany Lomax*
Oak Park, Illinois

The ideal man is one who's strong enough to be sentimental; secure enough to be spontaneous; intelligent enough to be imaginative; brave enough to be bashful; charming enough to be chivalrous; humble enough to be humorous; open-minded enough to be optimistic; romantic enough to be respectful; faithful enough to be free; candid enough to be committed; polite enough to be patient; classy enough to be confident; and rich enough to be revered.

——*Pamala E. Jackson*
Columbia, South Carolina

My ideal man treasures life and respects death. He remembers that as long as you are breathing, all things are possible.

——*Katrina E. Govan*
Brooklyn, New York

It isn't about how pretty his face is when he looks into the mirror. It's about how real his soul is when I look into his eyes. His honesty is the essence of his existence.

Tears don't steal his manhood, because his strength resides in his mind and soul.

His wisdom, his spirituality, his culture, his past, his present, his future— everything is a continuous discovery. His mind is armed with education, his heart is armed with charity, and his will is armed with integrity.

His love is constant even through the storms, yet it never overwhelms or robs you of your being. He's neither afraid to love too deeply nor ashamed of his confidence in that love.

This is a man of imperfection and a man of many flaws, yet every day with him seems like a new dawning, because the more you know, the more you love... and then you realize that his very existence is worthy of love's purity.

—*Tiana Jonelle Herbin*
Greensboro, North Carolina

The Perfect Man

Sit back, take a deep breath.... .
Exhale and dream.
He's my first friend, my partner in the "Big C"—
Commitment, confidence.
He's humorous with intelligence,
safe and warm.
He's romantic but not sappy.
Brilliant in spirit,
alive with life... an optimist.
His body may change, but never his heart.
The love of my life is learning daily,
He's my son...
and won't be ready till the year 2014...
at the earliest!!!

Thank me later.

——*Bobi McKeever*
Grand Rapids, Michigan

Cares enough for himself to keep up his appearance, but
knows that looks, including mine, don't make a relationship.
Has enough self-esteem that he doesn't have to put me down
to keep himself up.

——*Jania D. Powell*
San Francisco, California

My ideal man is Christ-centered... a trusted best friend... a passionate lover... a good listener... an honest communicator... an adventurous companion... a keeper of secrets... a protector of memories... an encourager of dreams... a compassionate helpmate... a gentle consoler... a loving support system... my partner in prayer... a respected role model for children... committed to our relationship... an undying love affair... the man my parents prayed I'd find... .

—*Carmen Avery*
Birmingham, Alabama

Limitless communication and, without a doubt, "it" can be worked out!

—*Dannie M. Herron-Willis*
Dallas, Texas

What the outside world thinks is not important because our world is where he flourishes and knows he has the security to reveal his true self. When I touch him he responds with a knowing receptivity.

—*Alicia K. Dixon*
Compton, California

Lines To ____

O come to me in my dreams love!
 When the world is wrapped in sleep,
And the silver moon like virgin queen,
 Her lonely vigils keep.
When all is hushed in calm repose—
 The earth, and sky, and sea,
Then hasten love to this far-off land,
 And dwell one hour with me...
O, do not forget to come, love,
 But on rosy pinions haste,
And deluge my willing ear, with
 Mementoes of the past,
And tell me, too, of that distant land,
 Its sunshine and its flowers;
And in return my strain shall be
 Magnolia's bright bowers.
Ah, do not fail to come love,
 For I'll woo my slumber to-night;
I'll lay me down to sweet repose,
 And wait for thee and light.
Then hie to my bower on wings of love,
 Ah, linger not by the way,
But solace this heart and bid it hope,
 For the dawn of a brighter day.

Mary Weston Fordham
1897

Son Of The Sun

Son of the Sun
who is my father, friend, lover wrapped in one.

Son of the Sun
whose widespread arms stand for passion,
protection, and peace.

Son of the Sun
whose smile radiates energy and healing that fuses to
ignite love that burns endlessly in my soul.

Son of the Sun
whose kisses are like butter, melting gently, sweetly,
rapturously on my lips.

Son of the Sun
who in wisdom accepts differences and doesn't pit one
against the other.

Son of the Sun
who is not afraid to kiss and dance with me, the moon
basking in the sweet ebony from our balance, while
touched by the light of our union— a sensuous eclipse.

——*Djana F. Harp*
Chicago, Illinois

Believes in a higher power. Loves himself, easily loving others. Knows family is important. Is romantic. Says "no" in a gentle tone. Sexually expressive with minimum hang-ups. Lives the meaning of honesty. Loves children. Left his ego back in his adolescence years. Likes to mediate. Lives each day as if it's his last. Likes seeing the sun set. Willing to take a risk for true happiness. Looks into my eyes.

—*Nicola Kelly-Jackson*
New York, New York

Recipe For Mr. Right

Take an honest, respectable man
Mix in several cups of tenderness and humor
Add a large portion of love for God, family and good jazz
Spoon in plenty of good sense
Remove any lumps containing fear of a woman with a good
    mind and an opinion
Sprinkle on one sexy smile
Bake in the warmth of my arms for as long as it takes
He's ready when he knows life wouldn't be the same
    without me

—*Pamela Byrd*
Pittsburg, Pennsylvania

The ideal man is a man who is cloaked in God's glory, unafraid to reveal his heart to others. He is a true man of integrity. An ideal man is really not as much a rarity as we convince ourselves that he is. He knows that love doesn't pay the rent. Often, he is present in men we pass daily without a second glance.

—*Ebuni JuJuan McFall*
Charlotte, North Carolina

The ideal man is a God-fearing confident man. He takes the time to keep his appearance up, while understanding that beauty is internal as well as external. In relationships, he is stern and stands his ground; yet he remains passionate and knows how to make a woman respond.

—*Neferterri Johnson*
Colorado Springs, Colorado

What Would You Do If You Met The Ideal Man?

A man who strides into your life with the confidence of a well-trained warrior going into battle;

A man who possesses the same strength in body, character and mind;

A man solid in build, firm in his goals, and unyielding in his life's pursuits;

A partner to Eve who feels the need for a spiritual guide in his life;

A being so gentle in nature that the spoken word never bruised, but smoothed the jagged edges of your soul;

A man molded in the image of God, reared by the teachings of those who came before him, and eternally reveres the one who gave him life;

An optimist who thrives on the joys of today, learns from the hurts of tomorrow, and never grieves the losses of yesterday;

A man you can really call "friend," a friend you can truly call "lover," and a being gifted enough to qualify as both;

A man who doesn't fulfill what you don't already have, but acts as a supplement;

A man whose only regret in life is that he didn't find you sooner;

...and as he walks toward you, the strongest of your secret senses tingles with the knowledge that you have found what once before you thought never existed.

—*Amie M. Morehead*
Washington, D.C.

Appreciates you
Brags about your cooking
Contributes to your inner growth
Down-to-Earth
Educated
Faithful
Goes shopping with you
Has values
Is secure
Jack of all trades
Knows God
Laid-back
Makes suggestions, not demands
Needs no improvements
Often compliments without hesitation
Prays
Qualities of a gentleman, he possesses
Respectful of others
Surprises you just because
Trustworthy
Uses "we" frequently
Very spiritual
Well-spoken
X-tremly intelligent
Your soul mate
Zealous attitude towards life

There may not be an ideal man per se, but he is perfect if
he is tailor-made for you!

— *Sharon Rene Davis-Mable*
Detroit, Michigan

A man who is comfortable enough with his sexuality and identity that he does not feel that he has to tear mine down. A man who can see me for who I am, the positives and negatives, and still loves me unconditionally. A man who honors and loves people regardless of their race, sex, age or sexual preference. A man who feels comfortable around children and can find it in his heart to play with them and to try to understand them. Someone who supports his elders and gives them the respect they deserve. A man who knows that God put mankind on this earth and that only He has the right to judge.

—*Jemilope Fasoye*
Brooklyn, New York

The ideal man would be an explorer of life and all it has to offer. He would:

Be Spiritually Grounded— the foundation to place his faith.

Respect His Mother And All Women— the bearers of life, the ultimate sacrifice.

Be A Role Model For Children— yours, mine and his.

Have A Solid Work Ethic— does his best.

Be Strong, But Sensitive— will be a rock as well as the soft sand; confident but not cocky.

—*Kim Spencer*
Mays Landing, New Jersey

Eight

Romance, Sex, and Good Looks
Romantic | Good Lover | Sexy | Good Grooming

A touch as soft as satin. Soft, plush, sensuous lips. Kisses
that delight and evoke the experience of eating cherry-filled
chocolate cordials. Caresses— soft, whispering and gentle. A
man who teases, pleases, and gets the job done.

With these women, lovemaking need not always be soft and
slow like a will-o'-the-wisp on a slow, lazy summer's day. It
can also be hot, steamy, and fever-pitched when the mood is
right, the senses are impassioned, and mutual trust has been
established.

Some of the women in the following passages speak of the
physical aspect of relationships. However, many more speak
of their longing for men who know that sex is not the only
avenue to intimacy or the only way to express love. They
long for men who are able to respond to a woman's need to
feel good about herself when she is with her partner. They
need to feel special, loved, and desired by their men. A man
who understands this about a woman holds the key to sharing her heart and mind as well as her body.

The women also feel that a man should attend to his appearance. No "fly-boys" please. No "Denzel looks" required. The ideal man will simply let his outer self be an expression of his inner beauty.

A man who knows how to maintain what the Creator has granted him is perfection regardless. All physical types are appreciated. Coarse hair, dark like midnight and tangled like sable cotton. Skin, with an ebony glimmer or a chocolate mocha hue. Thighs, arms, and chest, hard in some places, soft in others. Tall or short, muscular or lean, it's a woman's individual standard of beauty that rules. Thoroughly African, thoroughly male, and thoroughly delicious to taste and touch.

Standing confident, strong, ambitious; the ideal man exudes a sensuality appropriate in public. In private, he is relentless in bed. He loves tenderly. His touch—unselfish and concerned. Everything about him says he knows who he is; a man's man who likes being his woman's man. His woman—intelligent, beautiful, independent—knows his need to take care of her. Living with respect, calm, and perseverance; he amuses, pleases, and gets the job done.

—*Tia Hairston-Edwards*
New Haven, Connecticut

My ideal man is the one who can keep my heart beating at a smooth and steady pace. One who will take the beautiful moments we experience at the beginning of our relationship and stretch them over a lifetime.

—*Yvonne Butchee*
Willowbrook, Illinois

A man who knows how to "sex me" mentally and physically. He knows that "the job" is not done until we're both "singing" in unison. In this day and age, I want a real man not a fantasy... .

—*Jennifer D. White*
Jamaica, New York

111

He is the man who can hold his sexual "mack-selling" attitude back and accept friendship before courtship. He is the one who loves to explore my body and my life, and to kiss as if he's eating a chocolate cherry cordial.

—*Tamaya Reid*
Jersey City, New Jersey

Calls My Name

The ideal man is quick to smile and slow to anger.
Doesn't fear commitment, he demands it.
Is not intimidated by my strength, he depends on it.
When all eyes are on him, his eyes are on me.
He has the strength of a mountain,
But handles my heart with the gentleness of sand.
He makes love with the passion of a raging storm,
And calls my name during the power of his "thunder."

—*Gloria J. McGibony*
Cocoa, Florida

Handsome is not what it's all about. To me, he can be rough but not worn, and tough but not scarred. Risqué in ways we both can endure, most of all enjoy. Oh, the joy of a well-groomed man with casual attire, and a suit when necessary.

—*Greta Chatmon*
Baltimore, Maryland

For many, the ideal man would be a combination of film and music personalities. But for those in touch with reality, fictitious characters are a bust. As for myself, the ideal man would have a statuesque physique that towers over me and possess soft, plush lips that hide a smile that could brighten the darkest night. Hypnotizing ebony eyes, a sense of humor and a job are an absolute must. And a true believer in God is a plus.

—*Lynn Morrow*
Fort Worth, Texas

When he loves me, it's so complete that I can think of nothing else for days on end. His kiss is so tender and passionate because he does not focus on his own gratification but commits to the very essence of lovemaking— touching, feeling, holding, caressing and kissing.

When his lips meet mine, I drift into an island of calmness, warmth and peace. When I am with him, we are one. I embrace him, I cherish him, and thank God daily for allowing me to be blessed with the experience of loving this man.

—*Daphne Janice Skinner*
Tulsa, Oklahoma

A considerate, skillful lover with a killer smile. A great kisser, who sends roses "just because... ." Strong, independent, ambitious, honest, a good listener. Able to communicate his feelings. Spiritual, forgiving, at peace with himself. A best friend. Comfortable to be with, and makes me laugh. Able to appreciate and respect my womanhood, knows his weaknesses, admits when he is wrong. Loving, caring, faithful. Neat in appearance, takes care of himself. One who gets up for midnight feedings.

— *Name Withheld*
Chandler, Arizona

Single, Straight, and Ready!

— *Lisa Truitt*
Baton Rouge, Louisiana

His skin is black, as black as coal.
His hands are rough and scarred from life's work.
His hair is coarse, tangled like cotton.
With shoulders as broad as the sea.
His head held high with confidence and pride.
Eyes facing the future he cannot see.

— *Elizabeth Wilson*
Memphis, Tennessee

When a brother is beautiful within, all that he does for himself or others is reflected in that. My ideal man isn't one who dons the latest apparel, keeps a tight hairdo or has a smooth ride. Guys like that are a dime a dozen. Good looks are a definite plus, but I'll choose depth and personality over well-honed looks any day.

I'm not "knocking" fine brothers. I'm applauding all men who beautify themselves inwardly first.

—*Helen Jones*
Osceola, Arkansas

Attentive without claiming sole possession, he is expressive with a hint of flirtatious charm—just enough to keep the mystique but not so much that it invites distrust.

He gives back rubs at the right time with the tenderness he'd show his newborn child. He massages temples with a purpose; his fingertips acknowledging the stresses of your everyday life.

He knows not just your body but your mind and soul too. Yet, he takes time to discover the new joys you create in yourself each day.

—*Teresa B. Ingram*
New York, New York

Invitation To Love

Come when the nights are bright with stars
Or when the moon is mellow;
Come when the sun his golden bars
Drops on the hay-field yellow.
Come in the twilight soft and gray,
Come in the night or come in the day
Come, O Love, whene'er you may,
And you are welcome, welcome.

You are sweet, O Love, dear Love,
You are soft as the nesting dove.
Come to my heart and bring it rest
As the bird flies home to its welcome nest.

Come when my heart is full of grief
Or when my heart is merry;
Come with the falling of the leaf
Or with the redd'ning cherry;

Come when the year's first blossom blows,
Come when the summer gleams and glows,
Come with the winter's drifting snows,
And you are welcome, welcome.

Paul Laurence Dunbar
1917

———————————

My ideal man possesses the face and body of Tyson Beckford, the sexiness and lyrical wit of LL Cool J, and the sensuous voice of Maxwell. He has a wicked sense of humor but a very caring nature. He's strong and forceful but not overbearing. He knows how to tease me, please me, and make me feel loved. He knows what he wants and goes after it. Most importantly, he treats me like the woman I am.

— *Deanna L. Berry*
Rodeo, California

Smooth chocolate skin. A beautiful bald head. Strong hands. Sculptured arms and chest, thighs hard and strong, and a butt so tight and firm you just have to have a hand-full. A hint of a stomach that makes him a reality, not a dream. His hands and arms would hold me so tight, I could close my eyes and imagine that sweet smooth chocolate all over me.

— *Elaine Paige*
Westland, Michigan

My ideal man will have the mouth to tantalize my brain, the eyes to look into my heart, the nose to catch my breath, the ears to listen to my heart beat, and a touch as soft as satin.

— *Estella R. Turner*
Merced, California

Rich Dark chocolate,
no cream.
Tall in stature,
long and lean.
Slightly robust, yet
physically fit.
Love handles...
... that's it!
Smart about issues and
on the scene.
Loving,
about simple things.
Integrity
to do what's right.
An unattached man— all day,
not just at night.
Looks are nice,
personality too.
Outside in
will never do.
I expect the best
from God, you see.
Holy and blessed to stand in the gap
and love *me* to eternity.

— *Sharon Elizabeth Martin*
Pensacola, Florida

Strong face. Beautiful smile. Warm eyes. Broad shoulders. Strong back. Arms that shelter. Tight glutes that give jeans a nice definition. Looks good in everything and nothing. Makes long, intense love. Willing and able to communicate his feelings. Strong belief in God. No time for pettiness. Gently loving, confident enough to let sista be. Capable and self-sufficient even before I entered and made his world complete.

— *Deanna M. King*
Denver, Colorado

Mr. Right is the lover extraordinaire
He trusts that I won't cheat and I know he wouldn't dare
The sound of his sweet, seductive voice arouses me
Because he knows every inch of my body

—*Jennifer F. Bogar*
Newark, New Jersey

My ideal man would be clean-cut, and smooth-shaven. Skin color: caramel, dark brown, red-boned, or light. Hair texture: dreadlocks, bald, wavy, curly, or faded. Eyes: any color as long as they are real. Like Mike Tyson, the fighter, he has a well sculptured body. Like Stephen King, the writer, he has a vivid sense of imagination.

—*Regina Gray*
N. Las Vegas, Nevada

My ideal man would be: Bill Cosby (fatherly), Denzel Washington (yummy), Wesley Snipes (yessss), David Justice (have mercy), Kirk Franklin (heavenly), Malik Yoba (ooh baby), Eddie Murphy (funny), Keith Sweat (sing to me baby), Bill Gates (filthy rich) and Michael Jordan (Mr. Everything) all rolled into one!

— *Donna Clark*
Las Vegas, Nevada

He knows my body by heart. He can set the mood without saying a word. In one touch, I know he is mine and I am his.

— *Geri Wimley*
Kansas City, Missouri

He is a man who listens and understands; one who shares his own thoughts while holding your hand. He's the type of man whose presence is felt once he steps into a room. He's sensual, honest, strong yet gentle, and oozing with sexiness, all rolled together. Of course, it can't hurt if he's drop dead gorgeous too!

— *Stephanie Fennell*
Parlin, New Jersey

One who has distinguished height, smooth, soft glowing skin and persuading, dazzling eyes. His smile melts stones and his perfectly shaped head, catches your eye in an instant. His medium-sized, muscular body is lined with remarkable images describing his humor, sensitivity, charisma, intelligence, roughness and faith in the Almighty God. He is breath-taking and mind-blowing.

—*Jameka Duncan*
St. Croix, Virgin Islands

... And oh, yes! He must have big, juicy lips.

—*Dara Falayan Lovett*
Philadelphia, Pennsylvania

One who is always there for me whenever I need him. One who brings positive changes in my life. One who listens to me. One who adores me like a princess. One who remembers my birthday and our anniversary. One who gives love to cherish, and his shoulder to cry on. One who stops at nothing to tell me how precious I am to him and that I am his jewel of inestimable value. A gentle man to the core and a practical man forever.

—*Grace Ilonuba*
Riverdale, Georgia

Nobody's Lookin' But De Owl And De Moon
(A Negro Serenade)

De river is a-glistenin' in de moonlight,
De owl is set'n high up in de tree;
De little stars am twinklin' wid a sof' light,
De night seems only jes fu' you an' me.
Thoo de trees de breezes am a-sighin,
Breathin' out a sort o' lover's croon,
Der's nobody lookin' or a-spyin',
Nobody but de owl an' de moon.

Nobody's lookin' but de owl an' de moon,
An' de night is balmy; fu' de month is June;
Come den, honey, won't you? Come to meet me soon,
W'ile nobody's lookin' but de owl an' de moon.

I feel so kinder lonely all de daytime,
It seems I raly don't know what to do;
I jes keep sort a-longin' fu' de night-time,
'Cause den I know dat I can be wid you.
An' de thought jes sets my brain a-swayin',
An' my heart a-beatin' to a tune;
Come, de owl won't tell w'at we's a-sayin',
An' cose you know we kin trus' de moon.

James Weldon Johnson
1917

My Mr. Right Would Have:

Beautiful eyes:	to see my inner beauty;
Soft lips:	to whisper sweet nothings in my ear;
A healthy heart:	to give me the love I deserve;
A broad back:	to shoulder the weight of our burdens as People of Color in America;
Long arms:	to hold me as he tells me that everything will be okay; and
Strong legs and feet:	to Electric Slide our way into old age.

—Mirna E. Martinez
Bronx, New York

His voice makes me tremble with delight. The man that has this effect on me touches me like no other.

—Bonita C. Blackwell
Newark, New Jersey

He protects and cherishes his Nubian princess in every way. He is a man who can appreciate the pleasure of sharing a starry night or a breathless sunset. He is the man who can make the magic last forever plus a day.

— Sharron McDonald
Durham, North Carolina

The image of the ideal man means something different to each woman. He can be someone who can take your breath away with a glance or your fears away with an embrace. For me, it's not the pretty package that counts but what's on the inside.

— *Stacy Jackman*
St. Albans, New York

He's calm as an ocean, smooth as waves.
He's a chocolate desire every woman craves.
He makes wanting him a need, not a choice.
My heart skips a beat at the sound of his voice.
He's everything God wanted a man to be.
This ideal man, is the man for me!

—*Latrell Marie Wilson*
Travis AFB, California

As for the physical appearance, if it is pleasing to the woman, then he is the ideal man.

—*Patricia L. Perkins*
Sacramento, California

Intimacy takes time. It is a process. It needs to be fed, valued, nurtured, and allowed to grow. When we try to manipulate intimacy, we kill it.

Living for the moment, Mr. Right needs to love each moment, and the energy of the moment will spread beyond all boundaries.

—*Marietha J. Slade*
Chesapeake, Virginia

He'll make me feel beautiful even though I am not.

—*B. Felicia Morant*
Durham, North Carolina

The ideal man is an individual that will spend his free time with you— laughing, listening and learning his princess. The ideal man will search the world to find her, but on that given day, his heart will be filled with an electric emotion— one that only a princess can ignite. The ideal man could love this woman forever, making marriage the only answer.

—*Salundia Yarbough*
Ypsilanti, Michigan

Affection is not a problem with my Mr. Right and he shows it with love taps and tender kisses, rather than constantly demanding sex.

—*Kimberly L. Anderson*
Passaic, New Jersey

He is an incredible lover and he calls me "baby" the way no man can call his woman. He is my Black man. He likes nice things but is not obsessed with materialism. He finds creative, but never nefarious, ways to acquire them.

—*Martenia Blackburn*
Hayneville, Alabama

He must be slender, tall, with a *healthy* "six-pack."

—*Belinda C. Davis*
Clarkston, Georgia

He would be a candy-giving, flower-sending proud Black man. He would write inspired poetry, would truly love me, and he would be mine.

—*Juanita Green*
New York, New York

Well-groomed facial hair
Outlines sensual, friendly lips
His muscular torso tapers
To sexy-n-slim hips

Obvious strength beneath
A tender touch, a gentle kiss
He aims to keep me
In continual bliss

But for successful romance
Finance is a must
Entertainment, dates, travel
Outweigh physical compulsion and lust

God by his side
Guiding daily action
His outward calm stems
From inward satisfaction

Responsible and faithful
He lacks a roving eye
Lucky for me, my man
Is my ideal guy!

—Tamera Yvette Anderson
Nashville, Tennessee

He has two strong shoulders; one to lean on and the other to cry on. He has two strong hands; one to hold you and the other to help carry your bags after a day of power shopping. A passionate, tender lover concerned with your satisfaction as well as his own in those intimate moments.

—*Deidrah Thomas*
Detroit, Michigan

Five feet nine inches tall, weighing 170 pounds, chocolate in complexion and just as sweet. Pearly white teeth and a gorgeous smile. He makes going grocery shopping a pleasure and doing laundry a peach. He can outdo Chef-Boy-R-Dee and he outruns the Energizer Bunny. That's my ideal man.

—*Ingrid Falloon*
Stone Mountain, Georgia

He loves, respects, and cherishes his lady love like raw silk. He caresses with delicate hands and tender touches. Love is a two-way street and he is not afraid to do some walking.

—*Anastasia McGahee*
Chicago, Illinois

I would describe the ideal man as someone like my best friend. He is an attractive 5' 9" sexy man with smooth ebony skin, gorgeous white teeth that radiate in his beautiful smile, a clean-cut beard, broad shoulders and a hairy chest. He is well-educated and loves to learn new things. He lives with passion for his dreams and goals. He is kind, yet firm, supportive and an excellent listener— qualities that are important for a husband and a father.

He yearns for the simple moments in a relationship that include hugs that say, "I believe in you and I know you believe in me." In love, he is sensual and romantic and knows how to make a woman feel beautiful and special. Most of all, he is continually growing stronger in his walk with God.

——*Renee Rolling*
Chamblee, Georgia

He hits my funnybone, yet inspires me with his strength and integrity when he shares his aspirations. This sensuous lover provides unconditional love, unlimited hugs, and genuine passion that sends my heart racing; he then chases and catches my heart with compassion, gently caressing it back to calmness. Confident enough to respect my independence, he trusts me with his own heart.... Then he smiles beautifully.

——*Deborah M. Davis*
Detroit, Michigan

His eyes are kind and see beyond the superficial.
His ears listen carefully with full attention.
His hands like to touch gently, tenderly, often.
His mouth speaks truthfully, articulately.
His smile is quick, warm, and natural.
His legs can climb ladders, but prefer walking their
    own path.
His job— be it art collector or garbage collector— he
    does well, he does with joy.
His heart holds the boundless love of a considerate,
    compassionate man.

—*Rogena Walden*
Cartersville, Georgia

A midnight warrior standing tall and firm
His skin's as smooth as silk as it glides against your body
His eyes, the deepest shade of brown
Looking... deep into your soul
He is gentle and warm and understands your needs
Never once forgetting that you're all the woman he needs
He talks openly and honestly, rarely does he lie
But when he does it's only so you don't cry
He's man enough to know what to do
When he doesn't let his ego shine through
He puts it on the back burner
So he can learn how to please you and make you yearn.

—*Tiffany Marshall*
Oakland, California

Nine

Strength In Character

Strong Character | A Survivor | Self-Assured
Intelligent | Street-Smart | Common Sense
Responsible | Afrocentric | Maintains Dignity
Service To Community

An ideal man is a strong man. Not necessarily a man with bulging muscles, mighty arms and powerful thighs. But a man with strength of mind, an abundant heart, an insatiable quest for knowledge and an unwavering moral code.

A strong man is empowered by his worst experiences rather than overwhelmed by them. He has the ability to dig deep within when life seems like an endless series of trials. He makes the best choice for the welfare of his family when the only choices are between bad and worse.

A strong man is able to survive life's disappointments. Disappointments of his own making or of a society that professes fairness but frequently fails to live up to its own proclamations. He is hopeful enough to greet each new day with optimism. Yet, he is wise enough to learn from his mistakes and from those that walked the same path yesterday.

A strong man has the wisdom born of experience and the intelligence born of a continual quest for knowledge. He knows that he is a citizen of a great people who have built mighty kingdoms.

A strong man realizes that as essential as he is to our collective existence, he is but one link in a chain of life that must continue for our children. Yes, he protects his own, cherishes life, and contributes to his community.

The ideal man is simply a perfectly imperfect individual open to improvement. Bold, pleasing lines define his physical space. His aura, so alluring and so appetizing that intoxicating visions of confidence and power envelop me. Inspire me. Aspire with me. We can be involved in evolving creativity and he will in all ways act responsibly. Quite simply, the ideal man is perfectly imperfect, dependably independent and madly in love with me.

— *Cheryl Williams*
Middletown, New York

His heart has not hardened from disappointments and heartbreaks, but he has learned from them and they have made him stronger. His life experiences have made him better, not bitter; whole, not fragmented.

— *Jo Ann Scott*
Paterson, New Jersey

He would actually listen to what a true virtuous Black woman asks for: an honest, hard-working, respectful, splendid, and surviving Black man.

— *Angela Marie McKendall*
New Orleans, Louisiana

He is completely connected to his maleness. Not arrogant, but knows his strengths and weaknesses. In strength, he accomplishes all he sets his mind to do. In weakness, he remembers "grace" will see him through. He does not need the constant stroking of his ego to make him feel like "he's the man." He already knows that he is a man. He realizes the injustice of society, but does not allow himself to become a victim.

—*Bedie A. Steele*
Herndon, Virginia

He loves himself, accepts himself, and *is* himself despite the opinions of others.

—*Chris A. Gumbs*
Bronx, New York

The ideal man is like a diamond. No matter what he encounters he still shines. He can be rough on the outside but is valuable because of what he possesses inside. He's a man of integrity and is to be treasured, for he knows the art of loving a woman's mind, not just her body. He's dependable and won't crack under pressure. Most importantly, if he's handled properly he will be loyal and sparkle faithfully.

—*Darcia Parham*
Boston, Massachusetts

*R*ecipe For Perfection

3/8 cup of honesty
1/2 cup of boldness
1/2 cup of understanding the plight of a Black woman
1/4 tablespoon of assertiveness
1/8 cup of strength
1/3 cup of humility

Add a drop of aggressiveness, mixed with open communication, a pinch of good looks (to taste) with a touch of romance (to taste) mixed together well. Bake till a medium caramel or a dark chocolate (according to what you like), and here you have the ideal man. Enjoy!

— *Sylvia A. Jones*
Marietta, Georgia

He puts all things— particularly negative experiences— in perspective, learns from them, and moves forward. When I find him, he's mine.

— *Melanie M. Chambers*
Dover, Delaware

He takes action to get closer to the goals he sets for himself, not allowing negative vices to lower his standards.

—*Bahiyyah Layton*
Sanford, Florida

He is not just any man, he is a Black man, an African man. He seeks the legacies of his heritage, the depth of his spirit, the wonders of God and what it truly means to love.

— *DuEwa M. Frazier*
St. Louis, Missouri

The ideal man is of African heritage and sports a full-kept beard. He has Zulu brown eyes, Ashanti cheeks and Ibo skin. He is not necessarily a college-educated man, but he is no dummy. He is street-wise, respectful to women, and a father to all his children— financially, emotionally and physically. He works each day he's able to work. For him, working is a matter of pride and self-respect.

— *Valerie Y. Pointer*
Philadelphia, Pennsylvania

Mr. Right comes in all colors, shapes and styles. To me he would have to be a bold, not cold brother, lean not mean, and true to himself and me. A jammer, not a slammer. My man! Not his mommy's (boy). A hard worker. Knows of his sexuality and what his sexual agenda is for himself and me. Is not afraid to be sensitive to my needs. I could write all day...

— *Alexa R. Ross*
Jacksonville, Florida

The Black, Kushite, Nubian, Negro, African-American, never nigger, buppie, homeboy, Black masculine, sexy, dark mocha chocolate, cafe au-lait, cashew, caramel, all sweet, sensitive, vulnerable, necessary, wanted, abused, misunderstood, chastised, castrated (yet strong), kind, a worthy partner, pillar, rock of stability. The Black man, can our community stand to lose him?

—*Jeannine J. Hunter*
Myrtle Beach, South Carolina

*W*ants a resolution
Comfortable with his Blackness
Feels connected to the motherland
Loves knowledge for knowledge's sake

—*Lynn J. Nicholas*
Denver, Colorado

Unselfishly, he gives back and contributes to the uplifting of others. He's not perfect, nor is he perplexed by that fact. He's secure enough in his manhood to understand his limitations.

— *Sheerene Whitfield*
Inglewood, California

He was tall, dark brown, magnificently built, with a beautifully modeled back head. His profile was strong and good. The nose and lip were especially good front and side. But his looks only drew my eyes in the beginning. I did not fall in love with him just for that. He had a fine mind and that intrigued me. When a man keeps beating me to the draw mentally, he begins to get glamorous.

I did not just fall in love. I made a parachute jump. No matter which way I probed him, I found something more to admire. We fitted each other like a glove. His intellect got me first for I am the kind of woman that likes to move on mentally from point to point, and I like for my man to be there way ahead of me. Then if he is strong and honest, it goes on from there. Good looks are not essential, just extra added attraction. He had all those things and more. It seems to me that God must have put in extra time making him up. He stood on his own feet so firmly that he reared back.

Zora Neale Hurston

Shout It Out To The Universe!
The Ideal Man Is A Black Man!

He may be as black as the night with coarse hair and thick luscious lips or bright as the sun with hazel eyes and curly hair, but he is still a Black man.

The ideal man is mentally and physically strong and secure in his manhood. He knows what he wants and is by no means afraid to step to me. He knows that he is the man (the king of the castle) but he doesn't have an abusive bone in his body.

The ideal man has a good, kind heart. He is not threatened by my success because he knows that when I excel, so does he.

The ideal man never takes my kindness for weakness. He knows that no man can take his place in my heart because we are so good to and for each other. He is by no means perfect, but neither am I.

—*Wanda P. Payton*
Baltimore, Maryland

I imagine him with the soul of a soldier who uses his honesty as an advantage and his confidence as a strategy. He would exist!

—*Angelina A. Hunt*
Los Angeles, California

He stands tall, proud and unafraid. His beauty radiates with every move he makes. He is guided by his beliefs and doesn't hesitate to show you love. His eyes are bright and full of dreams.

He feeds you with his looks and reveals his strength with your every gaze. His hypnotic stare allows you to see his every dimension. His touch is strong, yet sensual. The slightest feel of his hands gives you support and allows you to feel the love he has for you.

He listens attentively and nurtures your every thought. He encourages your growth and enhances your creativity. He speaks with truth and wisdom and never dominates a conversation. He accepts your criticism and validates your opinions.

He's a protector. He's a friend. He's a lover. He's the ideal man.

—*Janet Y. Huger*
Brooklyn, New York

This man must have enough love and respect for himself to have goals that he is working to achieve. Everything he needs and wants, he obtains honestly, because he is not too proud to work hard.

— *Crystaline Barger*
Springfield, Illinois

He honors his heritage by giving back to his community; experiences life and love by staying spiritually connected with a higher power. Experiences the universe by making continual strides toward achieving a high state of consciousness. The ideal man lives with a clear conscience, a calm spirit, and a "saved" soul.

—*Karen S. Waugh*
Columbus, Ohio

Close your eyes and imagine him standing there— tall, strong and proud. The masculine essence pouring from the depths of his inner soul, hovering over him like a mighty cloud. I would look at him and ask, "How could God have made something as perfect and as powerful as you?" So magnificent that the other man fights for control of his blue-eyed women since he can't compete with the power of the mighty, forever-lasting Black man.

— *Sheila V. Christion*
Dallas, Texas

Self-esteem and strong willpower are a must in handling life's problems that our Black men are confronted with on a daily basis.

— *Name Withheld*
Hillside, New Jersey

He knows who he is and stands up for what he believes. He's your support when you need him. He's respectful and strong, with common sense. Yes, he's compassionate, he soars with ambition, his heart's as pure as gold.

— *Shermiya DeAndra Mosely-Benson*
Ft. Lauderdale, Florida

The ideal man for any woman should be a man who can look beyond her past and see her potential. This man can be the responsible father her children need and want.

—*Joyce Walker*
Jacksonville, North Carolina

An individual in control of his "manhood." Independent enough to make responsible decisions and strong enough to progress despite the obstacles. Spiritually secure and aware, he must be faithful to himself before he can be faithful to anyone else. Common sense to know he must respect himself and others in order to receive respect. A giver— mentally, spiritually, emotionally. He fulfills. He's tenacious. He's real.

— *Debra A. Johnson*
West Palm Beach, Florida

My Husband's Birthday

So you've reached your thirty-eighth birthday,
And by many a varied road—
I see that your hair is a trifle gray,
But you've toiled with a heavy load—
Of life's care, and pain, and sorrow,
Upon your shoulders broad;
You have striven that each tomorrow,
Found you nearer to heaven and God...

Though many the changes your eyes have seen;
In these few fast fleeting years,
O'er the graves of loved ones (now grown green,)
You've shed many bitter tears.
On life's great sea your bark has tossed,
And adverse winds have blown,
And threatening clouds your skies have crossed,
Yet still the sun has shone.

Now down the stream of life you glide,
And steer toward setting sun—
May each day's close bring sweet repose,
As you think of the good you have done.

Josephine Henderson Heard
1890

Grew up knowing who he is, where he is going and that he is aiming for the stars. He has poise, self-respect, confidence, a great mind and a heart of gold. Tall enough to be seen and acknowledged. His walk says, "I have been trying and will continue."

—*Hazel Wilson*
Mt. Vernon, New York

He is self-assured. Reads. Can articulate his thoughts. Takes time to think. He can lead and he can follow. He knows how to listen. He knows right from wrong— he strives after right. He commits to the things he believes in. He commits to the ones he loves. He doesn't deceive those he does not love.

—*Carla Y. Jones*
Dayton, Ohio

The ideal man seeks to eliminate fear, anger and doubt from his life. He understands that to be the best father, husband, brother, son, friend he can be, he must truly accept and love himself. He realizes that he is made from the substance of an abundant universe and that therefore, he can have anything that he can possibly dream.

—*Joyce C. Forbes*
St. Thomas, Virgin Islands

We as a race of people have been punishing ourselves for so long, men have forgotten how to be strong and able-minded, and women have forgotten how to be women. Many of our people turn to alcohol and drugs to hide their pain. We have forgotten our values, we have forgotten our God.

I am a strong Black woman who is still searching for that one man. In my opinion, men don't stay because they fear responsibility. And women suffer the consequences. It's hard to find all the qualities that you'd like in one man, especially if you size men up by their outer appearance.

Ultimately, though, until we learn to accept ourselves, we will never get beyond where we are.

—*Priscilla Brown*
Oakland, California

He faces the reality of who he *is* without feeling less of a man. He understands downfalls are only stepping stones, not brick walls.

—*Pearl G. Bailey*
Bronx, New York

He conducts his personal and professional life with dignity and respect for himself and others. He is not perfect, but committed daily to putting his best foot forward while empowering others to do the same.

— *Deneen M. Hendrick*
Wilmington, Delaware

Reflecting on my past conversations with my sisters on what characteristics my Mr. Right should possess made me realize that I must possess those same qualities as well. There is a universal law which states that what you are, you will attract! I must ask myself, do I possess spirituality and a love for life? Do I have the peace, unspeakable joy and patience to deal with the adversity the world may greet me with at times? Can I be open and secure enough to see my mate achieve his goal and provide him with the quality time to renew his spirit?

Do I possess a kindling spirit to serve others? Have I grown to the point that my ego will not hinder my relationship with others in my life? Am I open to other people with children? Because he must be open to the two children the Lord has Blessed me with.

As I continue to take my life's journey, I have realized that love from Mr. Right can't be the blessing I desire if I do not have it within myself.

When I meet Mr. Right I must be a whole person, not a half person who will have to drain him of his energy to complete myself. If I am whole and possess the characteristics as stated above, then I will attract my Mr. Right.

—*Beverly Canady*
Newark, New Jersey

He has a gorgeous mind and I am "sprung" on his ideas and ambitions. He knows sex is mostly mental, not just a physical act. He doesn't fear relationships and commitment.

—*LaTrisha M. Williams*
Chicago, Illinois

He can be found only in an ideal world. In our men we can seek only what we are capable of doing or being. If we, as women, are in constant search of an ideal that we ourselves cannot achieve, then we are in search of the unattainable.

The ideal man faces a world that is forever changing and growing increasingly bitter. This man is willing and able to stand behind you, in front of you, and beside you through it all. My man will be willing to accept me for who I am and who I long to be. He won't be afraid to call me his friend, his lover, his wife, and most importantly, his partner in life. He won't pretend to know me or pretend to listen. He will extend a generous ear to all that I have to say. He doesn't have to be a man of title or money. Just a man who is willing to listen, love, and respect me just as much as I do him.

—*Virginia Williams*
Ft. Myers, Florida

Ten

Partner, Protector, Pamperer
Loves Her For Herself | A Good Friend
Brings Out The Best In Her | Helps Her Achieve Her Goals

A man willing to shelter a woman's soul when it becomes overwhelmed. A man willing to protect a woman in times when she is physically and emotionally hurt. Such a man offers the promise of a satisfying and fulfilling relationship to many of the women in these pages. He shares the good times— the conversations, the laughter, the intimacy and the romance— as well as the burdens and heartaches of life.

These women also value loyalty and friendship. A man who will love a woman in spite of her flaws and past failures, yet support her in her efforts to realize her full potential, satisfies this desire. Often weary from a hectic and stressful day, they appreciate men who are willing to do a little pampering to help them unwind and recharge for the next day. To them, pampering communicates affection by wrapping the relationship in ribbons of tenderness, playfulness and consideration. Also, men who appreciate the importance of working together toward a mutually agreed upon goal, as co-partners not adversaries, are considered ideally suited to women seeking long-term relationships such as marriage.

To these women then, an ideal man lets his woman know that she is an important and essential part of his life. The refrain "actions speak louder than words" accurately describes their sentiments. To be sure, they appreciate the power of loving words. However, for them, a truly enduring and healthy relationship depends on what he does, at least as much as, what he says.

He has successfully progressed from "me" to "us" in his concern for family, friends and those in need. He understands that his God-granted days on earth are insignificant unless he makes them meaningful. Therefore, he responds in kind by being productive.

His worth is measured in the way he loves and is loved; respects and is respected; encourages and is encouraged. His life is invaluable.

— *Sylvia V. Savage*
New York, New York

Mr. Right has the protective strength of a father. He is as innocent as the first boy who had a grade school crush on you. He has the defiance of your first teen attraction and the raw sexual magnetism of your lover. He is the man you married; showers you with tenderness and support and lets you know that you are all he needs to get by.

He is your brother, an equal, someone to laugh with or, a safe shoulder to cry on. His physical and financial status mysteriously blur when you discover a love that is mutual and unique. Mr. Right is "all that," but most importantly, he is your friend.

—*Yvette Cordova-Sital*
Bronx, New York

Something about him caught my attention,
but it's nothing the eye can see.
Beauty is only skin-deep,
barely illuminating this mystery.
As honey soothes a sore throat,
his voice comforts me.
Deeper penetration reveals
an intellect I love to feel.
Let's unwind
means tell me what's on your mind.
Good or bad,
he's concerned what type of day I had.
He listens, he's comforting and he's into me.
That's the ideal man, you see.

— *Ennis Harris*
Reno, Nevada

The ideal man radiates an inner strength that no outer adornment can suppress. I feel good about myself when we are together or apart. He looks into my eyes with no reservation and says, "I love you, baby."

— *Carmen E. Jordan*
Queens Village, New York

The ideal man for me is a man of respect, morals and values. He shares his wisdom, sincerity and intellect. He doesn't have to be fine, just rich in character. Every challenge to him is an opportunity for growth. A spiritual man who will catch my falling teardrops and hold my hands during difficult times. No, he is not perfect, but parts of him are excellent; the mere thought of this gentle man will warm my soul.

—*Juney Anderson*
Rochester, New York

He realizes that the most intimate thing two people can do is share their dreams.

—*Fontella M. McCarty*
Fairview Heights, Illinois

He cultivates your dreams with his insight, inspiration and love, embracing all that you are and aspire to be, without conditions and requests of sacrifice. Helping you to continue to celebrate your design of your life, instead of a compromise for experiences you'd not have chosen if not for his presence in your life. When he encourages those things that best express who you are each moment of your life, then you've encountered the ideal man.

—*Joni Peques*
Salt Lake City, Utah

Mr. Right doesn't have to have large money bags hangin' from one side or the other. He just needs to be able to back me up if I need him to invest in my future, along with enhancing his own. Mr. Right cannot have an airtight spaceship for me to inhabit, but he will let me grow and bloom into a beautiful specimen of life, like an orchid. And in turn he will need to be striving for positive goals for himself.

—*Julia M. B. Mauldin*
Kilgore, Texas

He shelters my soul. He is willing to place himself as a partner, supportive friend and lover in my life, striving to fulfill my wishes, my wants, my deepest needs.

—*Cheryl R. Free*
Columbus, South Carolina

When he smiles, I melt. When he laughs, I am happy. When he loves, I am impassioned and when he cares, I am the most considerate. He is a virtuous and spiritual brother with a positive outlook and scintillating eyes that look only at me. His charm, wit, and honesty— second to none. He is, after all; my prince, my keeper, my protector, my beloved, my hero, and my Mr. Right.

—*Fannyé W. Strickland*
Marrero, Louisiana

The ideal man strives to become your best friend. He is available at all times to talk, to listen, to bring happiness and to be supportive. He will talk through his anger with you rather than use his fists. The words "I love you" will be reinforced by daily romantic gestures. Finally, the ideal man must rely on a higher power to bring about a positive relationship through change, acceptance, love and unity.

— *Sonya Honore*
Brooklyn, New York

My ideal man does not have to be perfect, but perfect for *me.* He is someone who complements my lifestyle, character, spiritual awareness, aspirations and goals in life.

—*Kitara R. Newell*
Richmond, California

The ideal man is one who teaches me any of life's lessons at any particular point in my life. I have found that every dating experience, whether pleasant or unpleasant, has taught me things about myself and has molded me into the woman that I am today.

—*Renee Noreen Rawls*
Atlanta, Georgia

Antar Ibn Shaddad, The Black Arab Knight

According to the romantic tale of chivalry and love centered on the life of Antar, the revered and feared Black Arab knight who lived in the 6ᵗʰ century, Antar passionately professed his love for his cousin, Ibla, on numerous occasions in and out of battle:

> *I am Antar, in form like a lion, and I dread not the utmost fury of my foes... . In the dark shadow of my spear is my parentage; and my black complexion, when it is questioned, gives the reply... . [T]ell Ibla that, for her sake, I have encountered horrors of the most eminent hazard; that I have endured dreadful scenes, and have returned triumphant, and the foe, in terror of me, dared not to appear before me... .*

> *Never did I behold amongst the human race anything like Ibla; lovelier and more beautiful than the sun and moon. When she stirs, her graceful movements resemble the wave of the branch with its green leaves. O, I vow no other charms will I ever love in my life; never, whilst the world endures, will I ever fail in my fondness for her. Ibla is indeed a matchless nymph; thin loined and delicate waisted. Lover for her penetrates my heart and my entrails: it is as if the tears that flow down my cheeks could flow in blood. Away, away, never will I forget her love; no, never till I rest in my grave. She is my object and desire in every desert; never will I abandon her till the day of judgement.*

Story Based On The Life Of Antar Ibn Shaddad

The ideal man is someone who often puts other people's needs before his own. He is someone who'll buy brakes or tires for your car and say he'd rather make sure you're safe instead of buying something meaningless.

The ideal man will put his arms around you in your darkest hour, and know just the right words to say to make you truly believe everything's going to be all right.

——*Michelle Boyd Dover*
Spartanburg, South Carolina

I am not looking for a pliable man to mold,
But a confident, strong man who'd be the
mate to my soul.

A gent who revels in the ambrosia of a relationship
and all that it can be.
A man who is the wind that calms my raging sea.

He is romantic, patient and gives unconditional love.
Mr. Right could never be wrong when selected by
the omnipotent God above.

——*Berlinda Roquemore*
Frisco, Texas

Someone whom I could work with financially so that we can create a foundation and hold onto each other during good times and bad. Someone who wants to help me with my dreams and will allow me to help him with his. Someone who is patient, mild-tempered and cool, yet a warrior. Someone who is good in the bedroom and knows what to do or is willing to learn. A friend, a lover and someone who is not connected with an ex-love!

— *Selena M. Wade*
Yeadon, Pennsylvania

To me, an ideal man is the man with whom you can be yourself. The man who loves you despite your past, because of your present, and with hope for your shared future. The top priorities of the ideal man are: his spirituality, his family, and contributions to his community. To me, the ideal man can and will give of himself freely.

— *Penelope Luster–Downs*
Lincoln, Nebraska

A really good man can press out your hair! Knows how to cook, or fix a flat, tune up the engine, and do all that. A sharp dresser; phat, not fat. He loves my cat. Mr. Right, find me... .

— *Martha Dixon*
Los Angeles, California

It radiates from the light in his eyes and glows from his smile... he loves me. I am an important part of his life— his mate. I find comfort in his arms. Confidence, compassion and consideration are his trademarks. He is strong yet gentle, macho yet sensitive. He has entrusted me with his heart. He's the ideal man because he completes me, complements my life and is a part of my future.

— *Catherine Blacher-Cameron*
Hazel Crest, Illinois

Despite all the other women he has had or could have been with, he takes pride in the one he's got.

—*Michelle Nova Williams*
Athens, Georgia

The ideal man is one who holds his master plan in his heart and strives to create his own opportunities. When needed, he abandons the world and gives his undivided attention to his queen. His love sends chills and inspiration through her body. He is secure enough to appreciate her essence and couples it with arms stretched to catch her if she falls.

—*Aginah Smart*
Philadelphia, Pennsylvania

He has soft eyes, open ears, and an open heart. He doesn't compromise his beliefs or mine. He bends but never breaks. He watches my back. His words are gentle but firm. He gives me freedom and support enough to grow and to dream. He's brave enough to tell me when he's too weak to finish the race. His pride doesn't overshadow his love.

—*Angel M. James*
Istanbul, Turkey

The ideal Man Is:
    A dreamer to help me finish my dreams,
    A coach to prod me along,
    A doctor to heal my wounds,
    A contractor to rebuild my spirit,
    A friend with a soft shoulder,
    A massage therapist with nimble fingers,
    A shepherd to lead me home.
The ideal man:
    Raises his children high,
        so they can see the world and dream
        for themselves.
    Wants me to do the same for him.

—*Donna Hemans*
Hyattsville, Maryland

A Negro Love Song

Seen my lady home las' night,
Jump back, honey, jump back.
Hel' huh han' an' sque'z it tight,
Jump back, honey, jump back.
Hyeahd huh sigh a little sigh,
Seen a light gleam f'om huh eye,
An' a smile go flittin' by—
Jump back, honey, jump back.

Put my ahm aroun' huh wais',
Jump back, honey, jump back.
Raised huh lips an' took a tase,
Jump back, honey, jump back.
Love me, honey, love me true?
Love me well ez I love you?
An' she answe'd, "'Cose I do" —
Jump back, honey, jump back.

Paul Lawrence Dunbar
1902

Physical appearance may be important to some, but so many other qualities overshadow my ideal man's chiseled jaw line, athletic build and sparkling smile. He makes me laugh even when I want to scream. He, unquestioningly, is always there when I need him. He listens and communicates, and expects the same. When I doubt myself he believes in me and brings out my best with his loyalty, support and affection.

———*Dawn Cotter-Jenkins*
Jamaica, New York

*L*ike a chameleon,
his personality camouflages
my temperamental nature.
When I'm blue, he's a clown.
When I become fire-red with intense feelings,
he's the calm to *my* storm.
When I'm giddy with laughter
like splashes of yellow,
he's just as playful!
When I'm gray like a morning rain,
his strong arms become peaceful and cozy.
When I stare into his eyes,
intimate colors are reflected...
those of love and respect.
And *I* am fulfilled.

———*Donna Scantlebury*
Mississauga, Ontario

My Perfect Man: What Counts To Me

My perfect man will:

> Consider me his *number 1* person.
> Be *twice* as nice as anyone I've known.
> Have *3 times* my strength, be *4 years* older, 5' 6."
> Tell me he loves me *7 days* each week.
> Not place me "behind the *8-ball*."
> Stand by me *9 months*, telling me I'm still his
> *perfect "10."*
> Prefer my company Sundays to that of any *11-man*
> football team.
> Shower me with *dozens* of hugs and kisses,
> "just because... ."

Footnote: I guess when it all adds up, my perfect man would have to be just like the man I married. My husband, my best friend, my one in a million.

> — *Dori Swarbrick*
> *Laurel, Maryland*

The ideal man is a man who can see your flaws and your underdeveloped character, and love you in spite of it all. He is responsible enough to face and express his weaknesses and pains. Mr. Right works five days a week, provides for his family, takes pride in himself and in everything he does.

> — *Sheila Walker–Warner*
> *Columbus, Georgia*

An ideal man is a friend. He's always there, even when you don't want to be bothered. When you're physically and mentally hurt, he's there to help you overcome the pain. He's a special friend when you feel, need and want love. He's there for companionship or just in thought.

—*Macena S. Wright*
Rocky Mount, Virginia

My ideal man is someone that sticks by me through thick and thin, through good times and bad times. If I am too tired to make love, he'll cuddle instead. My ideal man shares my hopes, my dreams and aspirations. He encourages me to go that extra mile. He's willing to let me spread my wings and fly, knowing that I'd never fly too far away from his life.

—*Isadora Coger*
Charleston, South Carolina

The ideal man is cooperative. He is his woman's "right hand man." He is not without flaws (though we women may wish so), but his strengths far outweigh his weaknesses. Anyway, who would want a man so perfect that there would be little use for us?

—*Arneice Kimbro*
Lauderhill, Texas

He may see a woman that he thinks is prettier than I am and her butt may be bigger than mine, but at the same time he is confident that his baby at home loves him and that he doesn't have to go after that. He's content with me and builds on what we have.

——*Pamela Tatum*
Baltimore, Maryland

Willing to work together to reach our goals.
Willing to share household chores.
Able to communicate.
Able to express himself without violence.
Willing to accept me as his full-figured woman,
And climbing the highest mountain top
To shout to the world, that I am his woman!

—— *Saundra A. Giles*
Warner Robins, Georgia

A man who's not controlled by a materialistic world, but can surround us with the things we love and enjoy. He can take the good with the bad and find understanding in both. He believes in a higher power.

——*Kimberly Lewis*
Birmingham, Alabama

He is a spiritual and accomplished man of few words. He delights in making me happy. He honors, cherishes and respects my mind and body. He is soft when he loves me, and hard when he protects me. We connect mentally and spiritually. His love for God, self and family drive him to be a better provider. He motivates me and appreciates my contributions. He is peace, love and happiness personified!

—*Janine B. Smith*
Lincoln Park, Michigan

A sincere, honest and dependable man who is not afraid to love and trust me. An open-minded man who will appreciate and support a strong, intelligent woman. A man who does not need a holiday to give me a dozen roses. A man that gives soft kisses and strong hugs. A man that listens as well as talks. Essentially, my ideal man would be a combination of my father, friends and past loves.

—*Bateacha Clarke*
Queens, New York

A man who can stand by his woman in her time of need, whether it be with a hug, a smile, or the simple line, "It'll be all right baby." A man who can show his true emotions and leave the "macho front" in the backwoods. A man who can share his opinions openly, but also appreciate when his loved one has a different view. Most importantly, the ideal man is one who shows family, friends, and strangers alike that there is no one else in the world that makes his life more complete than his soulmate.

—*Yolanda Brunson*
Brooklyn, New York

Eleven

The Family Man
Family Oriented | *Helps With Children* | *Helps Around House*
Responsible Father | *Good Provider*

The family is life sustaining, life supporting and, life defining. For the women in these pages, this statement holds true. The question is not whether the ideal man should have a family, sown by his own seed or "ready made," but whether he can be a responsible father to the children entrusted to his care and a loving husband to his wife.

To those seeking to fill the position of "family man," the faint of heart need not apply. A man's ability to be steadfast, loving and supportive has little, if anything, to do with his ability to procreate. If truth be known, being a family man is not always easy or enjoyable. The challenge is to be a positive role model for our children. In the following passages, women share their desire for men who will help guide our children toward fulfilling the promise of their heritage while steering them away from such pitfalls as alchohol and drug abuse.

If a man must be willing to do a little walking to sustain a loving relationship, he must be willing to run a marathon to reap the benefits of a loving family. Despite the challenges, the ideal man desires a family; indeed, he craves it. He knows that in receiving the gift of a family, he has been blessed. A wife's embracing love and faith. A child's unconditional and resilient love. A parent's unending pride and concern. These living gifts create an environment which nurtures self-esteem, fosters laughter, creates loving memories and gives us a sense of our place in the tapestry of life.

Sharp. Wearin' suits that ain't wearin' him! Fine. Tall, dark, handsome, not vain. The plight of his people on his mind. Fights injustice. Loves his job. Leaves at 5 'cause his kids come first, last, always. The shirt off his back is yours if you need it. But a doormat, he'll never be. Spiritual, educated, in love with his wife.

—*P. J. Baron*
Laurelton, New York

Takes care of his children from diapers to diplomas. Cherishing each moment he has with them and placing his family above all.

—*Charlotte Japp*
Garland, Texas

He's more than a shoulder to cry on because he knows how to comfort. He's not afraid of being "Mr. Mom" when you have to work late. He loves your children and lets them know that he's genuinely interested in them— not just their mother. When you're sick, he brings you chicken soup and lots of compassion.

—*Mary Greene-blade*
Ruston, Louisiana

My ideal man is spiritual. He believes in God, the Father and that he was made for a purpose. He cares about his world. He wants a family. He needs a wife who is a help-mate. He needs children— not only of his seed but any who need to be fathered.

——*Patricia A. Martin*
Jacksonville, Florida

My man takes care of his home
With the deepest respect for family.
He creates a sacred zone
Envisioning a future for "us" instead of "me."

——*Mila Stephens*
Detroit, Michigan

He would raise his children responsibly and with love be-cause he views them as our greatest treasures. As for his mate, he would treat her as his equal, not as his maid or punching bag. He would view life optimistically because he knows that although there are some rough times, joy always comes in the morning.

——*Tina Walker*
Indianapolis, Indiana

Excerpts From Private Spotswood Rice's Letter Of
Warning To A Slaveholder's Claim To His Daughter
(Benton Barracks Hospital, St. Louis, Mo., Sept. 3, 1864)

*... now I want you to understand that mary is my Child and she
is a God given rite of my own and you may hold on to hear as
long as you can but I want you to remembor this one thing that
the longor you keep my Child from me the longor you will have
to burn in hell and the qwicer youll get their for we are now
makeing up a bout one thoughsand blacke troops to Come up
tharough... and when we come... to the Slaveholding rebbels for
we dont expect to leave them there root neor branch...*

*... I want you to understand kittey diggs that where ever you and
I meets we are enmays to each orthere...*

*... now you call my children your pro[per]ty not so with me my
Children is my own and I expect to get them and when I get
ready to come after mary I will have bout a powrer and autherity
to bring hear away and to exacute vengencens on them that hold
my Child... I want you now to just hold on to hear if you want to
iff you conchosence tells that the road go that road and what it
will brig you to kittey diggs I have no fears about geting mary out
of your hands...*

An ideal man forges a secure environment with genuine interest and commitment. Although his eye may roam, his body, mind and soul rest with one woman. He supports his family with lawful activities that provide necessities and affordable wishes.

— *Dawn K. Guillory*
Lake Charles, Louisiana

If he has okay credit, works hard to take care of his family, spends time with the kids, has the patience and security to pursue his own dreams while encouraging his woman to do the same, he is, without a doubt, the ideal man. These are all qualities as rare as good looks are common.

— *Nicole D. Watson*
Oakland, California

He will possess intellect and integrity; constantly striving for self-improvement while empowering others. A preservationist for family, Christian and moral values. He embraces fidelity and honesty, reflecting his commitment to a lifelong relationship. A sensual and passionate lover, leaving behind toe-curling experiences.

— *Deidre O. Wilson*
Robersonville, North Carolina

Someone who can see beyond himself;
Can stand the rain, and bring the sunshine
   with him;
Who's there for his family;
Never tries, he does;
Doesn't need reassurance, he knows what is true;
Isn't insecure or afraid of sharing his love, thoughts,
   dreams, and fears;
Knows that the longest journey starts with the first
   step... and continues... one step at a time;
Knows that love is not a problem to be solved, but
   a gift to enjoy;
Is not afraid of looking beyond today;
Knows that love means giving one another space to
   be all that they are, and all that they are not.

——Jenell Bellamy
Philadelphia, Pennsylvania

The ideal man is not a handsome man, is not a well-built man, but a man I can have faith in and trust with our life, our children and our home.

The ideal man is not a well-educated man, is not a preacher man, but a man who has the knowledge and ability to take care of his well-being and the faith and trust in me to take care of mine.

——Jacqueline Smith
Kansas City, Missouri

Double the gifts your mother gave you and care for her as she cared of you. She bore a heavy burden in you and did not abandon you. When she brought you forth after your months, she was still bound closely to you. For her breasts were still in your mouth for three years. While you grew, she cleaned your filth without disgust in heart and without saying "O, what can I do?" She placed you in school to be educated and came there daily on your behalf with bread and beer for your teacher. Thus, when you become a young man and marry a wife and establish your house, lose not sight of your own childhood. Raise your children as your mother did you. Do not let her find fault with you, lest she raise her hands to God against you and God hear her complaints and punish you.

The Book of Wise Instruction
Retranslated from the ancient and sacred Egyptian writing

Mr. Right, with children, understands that raising children is a job for both parents. He helps with 100% of the household chores. He finds out for himself what is going on in the children's school and takes an active part. He doesn't leave homework "for the women," but realizes that both parents should try to make learning fun. He teaches family values, and listens to your children about everything that happened that day.

Mr. Right also understands that sometimes you need some quiet time alone and runs the bubble bath just for one! When you return to the bedroom, a special aroma fills the room, rose petals are all over the bed and then he just lies right next to you, puts his arms around you and the night ends with a sexy kiss.

—*Jeanette R. Haigler*
Philadelphia, Pennsylvania

He loves children and is a strong role model for boys. He chooses what's right over what's popular. He takes a stand, even if he's the only one standing. He adores me and isn't ashamed to admit it.

—*Marria Bratcher*
Oklahoma City, Oklahoma

Being the single mother of a three-year-old son, I need a brother my son can look up to. Someone my son can mimic without my skin crawling. He needs to be willing to help me guide my son into manhood.

— *Ursula LaFrance Anderson*
Jeffersonville, Georgia

Twelve

Voices of Experience
Wisdom From The Experienced, The Scarred, & The Healed

With each successive relationship, a woman reassesses the qualities a man should possess to satisfy her desire for a loving bond. Experience then, is key. In the following pages, women write of the promising potential of a good man. They share dreams that have been tempered by the wisdom of experience.

Some women share the lessons they have learned from prior marriages and identify the attributes a man must bring into a relationship to make it work. Widows share memories of cherished men no longer by their side. Married women contribute their thoughts by identifying those qualities that make for a solid relationship. And finally, there are single women who wonder if the sum total of their experiences with men is to be restricted to those who provide temporary comfort but little promise of a shared future.

Most people don't really appreciate the sweetness of life until they've tasted some of the bitterness life has to offer. I've been married once and had two serious relationships; all three left me with a bitter taste in my soul. The man I am with now makes me laugh, really listens to me, values my opinions, believes that communication and respect for one another are as important as love, is trustworthy, and believes he is answerable to God.

—*Tanya Morgan-Hicks*
Los Angeles, California

He is a mature man, not simply a person who has aged. One whose greatest accomplishments, after decades of existence, are not how much booze he can consume, how well he dances, dresses, or plays cards. My ideal man is a loving, confident, caring, mature gentleman.

—*Loretta Allison*
Temple Hills, Maryland

I have seen him only in my dreams. He's tall and sturdy like an oak tree. I look for clues and through his eyes I discover kindness, gentleness, and honesty. A man of respected stature in the community. A life balanced with pain and happy times. A smile to brighten any day. He, too, is looking for the ideal woman.... And we both wait!

—*Lorraine Carnes*
Hudson, Ohio

My ideal man is a mixture of many. From my father, I would take his wisdom (gained from life, not books) and his loyalty (married to the same woman for 57 years). From my brother would come perseverance (raised four children). Strength would come from my husband (to lean on when I'm tired). I would take the spirit of my five-year-old autistic child (can't talk but shares his world with me).

—*Jacqueline Sharp*
Cleveland Heights, Ohio

The ideal man, would be an African-American man, a true gentleman who still believes in opening doors for women. He would be old-fashioned— trustworthy, kind, honest, responsible, respectful, sensitive, personable, sharing. Must believe in God and prayer.

Down to earth, with a great sense of humor. He is a good communicator, employed, a non smoker, and drug and alcohol free (a social drinker). He would be affectionate, romantic, and enjoy the simple things in life.

—*Yvonne M. Robertson*
Columbus, Ohio

My past experiences with men have not been pleasant, to say the least. Like many other sistas, I've been through the ringer with them. I seldom date, and lately, I don't keep company with a man any longer than it takes to finish a meal. It's hard to trust them. But I do enjoy male company.

I had pretty much decided that I was destined to live out my remaining years on this earth, on the dating scene. I figured as long as I could keep *It* up, I'd forever be asked out to dinner on a Friday night every once in a while. I don't get many dates, but enough, I guess, to assure me I still possess that enormous male magnet, *It,* whatever *It* is!

It seems to be something that men want and women have. I've been told on several occasions that I had *It*. Men seem to be ever pursuant of *It*. They are always looking for a woman who has *It*. I've over-heard them say "I've got to get *It*," or "she doesn't have *It* anymore."

It seems to be something a woman has when she first meets a man, but loses somewhere along the way after she gets him. Nevertheless, I suppose as long as I keep *It*, I'll be good for an occasional Saturday afternoon luncheon.

But who wants to go through life keeping *It* for the Friday night and Saturday afternoon guys. Aren't there brothas out there who want a faithful loving sista in their lives? Brothas who: understand that a relationship is a shared commitment, recognize kindness and can differentiate between that and weakness, accept the leadership role in a relationship without confusing it with male domination, and appreciate you for the precious life support system that you are! Where are they?

I meet brothas all the time at the gym, in the grocery store, even Church! Professional, educated, self-assured brothas who say they're burned out on the dating scene. Brothas who say they are sincere, only to find out in a very short period of time that their actions are not reflective of their statements.

I've always thought of myself as being quite an optimist! I have always believed that in the worst of storms, you should wait patiently. After it's over, you can always hear the birds sing if you listen. Even in a concrete jungle, the sky is still blue—just look up! For every horrific death, there is a miracle birth and then new life begins with joy! I really believe in this kinda' stuff! I really believe in the impossible! But I've been having serious doubts about brothas these days.

Through its peaks and valleys, life and relationships are wonderful. And it would be nice to share that thought with someone of the opposite sex. Not just over a glass of wine or between "ahhhh's," but all the time, for all time (or at least until we are both old enough for dentures).

Maybe my time will come, maybe not. I'll continue to do the Friday night and Saturday afternoon thing with brothas who are in pursuit of *It*.

I can't help myself, I enjoy male companionship and I suppose you have to tread those shallow streams to get to the river.

—*Ki' Lora*
Kansas City, Missouri

For 33 years, he has been there for me. He is the father of my children. He is strong yet sensitive, wise and caring, and he is my husband, my lover and my friend. He understands me and my needs. I have found the ideal man in my life. A good man, who has a good woman.

—*Dianne France*
Laurelton, New York

Mr. Right is a man who respects his woman as well as himself. A man who truly believes in family values with his heart and soul. He will do anything to keep his family intact. He will always make his woman feel loved, wanted and very much needed. This is definitely a man who can satisfy his mate a complete lifetime, without chasing other women... after all, any "dog" can and will do that.

—*Bennie Prince*
Vancouver, Washington

After 30 years of living single, 14 years of endless dating, 10 years of soul searching and 3 years (and counting) of growing spiritually, I have carefully shaped my own opinion of Mr. Right.

Mr. Oh-So-Close-To-It

You look to God to lift you from lows
You love family, friends and foes
Your mother's face brightens when you're in view
Your siblings are eager to tell you what's new
No matter how complicated life may be
Comfort is always sought for and from me
With a touch that's gentle and warm
I know kindness is simply your norm
You always show how much you care
And "I love you" often fills the air.

— *NaTasha de Nia*
Louisville, Kentucky

He must be strong, straightforward, full of courage and integrity; embracing the world. A manchild born of the struggle, unafraid of the battle, wanting to win, able to love. This man. My man.

— *Dabura Karriem*
Brooklyn, New York

I must say that after all the relationships and two marriages, sensitivity is my desired characteristic in a man. Sensitivity would place him and keep him by my side during childbirth and child-rearing, overcoming the defensive attitudes Black women sometimes display to protect their feelings.

Having reflected on my strengths and weaknesses I feel that, for the most part, we as women want to remain and function in our roles, but we are forced to reside in places where we generally do not do well. To me, those places are: at the head of the family, as sole breadwinners, as both mother and father. I have been in all those roles and my children have done well, but it was not easy. Many women are in this same situation. But a sensitive man would recognize and appreciate a woman for what she is— a helper and a complement.

—*June R. Jerry*
Baltimore, Maryland

My idealism regarding men has waned somewhat at age sixty-two. My ideal man is Black, in my age group, unmarried and unaddicted. He has a passion for the simple things in life— a walk in the park, music, a good book, dancing, sports, good conversation and a good sense of humor.

—*Frances N. Pinckney*
St. Petersburg, Florida

My ideal man would be 6' 3" with Bill Cosby's charm and personality, Malik Yoba's build, Barry White's voice, Isaac Hayes' cool, Sam Cooke's singing voice, Ossie Davis' wisdom, Damon Wayans' sense of humor, Gregory Hines' dance fever, André Braugher's diction, Blair Underwood's good looks, Don Cornelius' attire, Malcolm X's fire, Dr. Martin Luther King's strength, and Jessie Jackson's morals.

—*Brenda J. Hall*
Bronx, New York

My Mr. Right's due any day
Comin' with all the right things to say
Full of style, brawn, and intelligence
Learned, but in possession of common sense
Tender, loving, daring, bold
Integrity, honor, soul shining like gold
Healthy, helpful, humorous, but no fool
A product á la the "old school"
Giving, deserving, with ability to feel
Passion enough to make memories seem real
Yes, Mr. Right, soon you'll see
Together *is* our destiny

—*J. Y. S.*
Columbus, Ohio

In a comic strip, a patron asks a waitress if the guy she is dating might be her Mr. Right. She replies, "No, he's just Mr. Right Now."

Hopelessness should not limit women to settle for a quick fix.

The Scripture says that man and woman must be equally yoked. If not, they will be pulling in opposite directions. The ideal man must also know the difference between holding a hand and chaining a soul.

He must plant his own garden and decorate his own soul— not wait for someone to bring him flowers.

Mr. Right must know that love does not mean leaning, that kisses are not contracts, and that company does not mean security. In other words, he must have self-confidence and self-esteem!

On the other hand, a woman must know that she has value. She must keep her head up, her eyes open and not settle for less. "Mr. Right Now" simply will not do!

—*Janita F. Middleton*
Southfield, Michigan

I am 35 years old, a paralegal student, a widow and single mother of an 8-year-old daughter. I have been a widow since my daughter was eleven months old.

I have met a whole lot of men but very few were ideal men. Here is my take on the ideal man.

> Fair, honest and truthful
>
> Capable of doing anything,
> but chooses to do the right thing
>
> Attends spiritual services or feels guilty
> about not attending
>
> Pays his child support willingly
>
> Does not let drugs, circumstances or anger
> control him
>
> Believes in monogamy
>
> Works every day and pays his taxes
>
> Does not live with females not born to him
>
> Has no hair where skin should be
>
> Tall, short, black, white or green
>
> The ideal man is one you can respect

> — *Deborah Stinson-Melton*
> *Long Beach, California*

I have been married for 21 years, my husband and I separated about a year ago. I'm the mother of 3 children— 25, 24, 23. I'm also the proud grandmother of six grandchildren.

My ideal man believes, trusts and loves God. He does not feel intimidated when his little boy plays with dolls or his little girl likes to play with a basketball or drive a truck. He's there for his children when they cry in the night and he loves his wife even if she has gained three dress sizes since their marriage.

He always finds time for them to sneak away and whisper "sweet nothings" in her ear.

—*Name Withheld*
Forrest Hills, Texas

Thirteen

More Creative Expressions
More Words With Spice & Soul

Written with soul and flavored with spice, women describe the qualities they desire in a loving man.

The proud tilt of his head. His sculptured body. His brilliant mind. His sage spirit. My name is sweet nectar on his lips. He holds my attention, in and out of the bedroom. Answers on the first ring if I'm out late. Feeds me my favorite ice cream after a hard day. Knows when I need a warm rosemary oil massage. Forgives me when I act like a complete idiot. Yeah, that's my ideal man.

—*Antoñietta A. Wilson*
Brooklyn, New York

*T*he Ideal Man Is...

Respectful:	he treats you as kindly as he'd treat his grandmother.
Loving:	he brings flowers just because.
Admirable:	he's the one your dad would choose for you.
Patient:	he encourages you through the 10th diet this year.
Moral:	he does what's right, even when no one's watching.
Responsible:	he provides all you need and most of what you want.
Passionate:	he makes sure you're satisfied first.

He's truly a gift from God!

—*Jammie Davis-Johnson*
Herndon, Virginia

He mirrors the mate he is looking for, complementing the lady he adores. His caring qualities bring him to his knees, as he asks for a lifetime commitment. His love is no mistake or accident. His pledge: a dedicated partner, a foundation, a friend, a lover. And if she already has children when they meet, he embraces them, loves them as his family.

Mr. Right is not easily found. But, just check where you're looking 'cause he's around.

—*Kecia M. Smith*
Copley, Ohio

I love a man who can tell a comedic story or a joke because I grew up with parents who did this daily. Humor keeps your life expectancy up, stress down, puts a positive glow on your face, and illuminates your soul.

Secondly, I know there is absolutely nothing as profound as a man who uses the gift of common sense. The gifts from the head, heart, and spirit taught by one's parents, grandparents, and the church are invaluable.

—*Valerie D. Parker*
Richmond, Virginia

He's grounded, rooted, solid, ordinary
Possessing self-love in order to give love
Regardless of life's setbacks or problems
He's looking to the inside for self-respect,
    self-assurance
Planning, aspiring, attaining
He accepts a relationship,
knowing it's not always fifty-fifty
Sometimes sixty-forty, sometimes seventy-thirty
But he continues to contribute
To grow in that relationship
And he doesn't mind being rescued
As he's been the rescuer

—*Melissa Chandler*
Atlanta, Georgia

Has God in his heart, and a genuine soul.
Continuously prepares for life's journey.
Realizes the courtship never ends.
Is a force to be reckoned with in business and
play and is a mental lover.
Balances life through prayer, preparation
and organization.
Uses his five senses as a means to positivity.
Has east coast work ethics, west coast ideas,
and southern values!

—*Nuria*
Chicago, Illinois

The B-ball Allegory

- Stands 6' 9" and commands respect on and off the *court*;
- Scores *two-points* for his belief in God;
- Voice *travels* as he spreads the word of God;
- Believes the best *defense* against pre-marital sex is abstinence;
- Spends his *time-outs* enjoying his family and encouraging our youth;
- Can *slam dunk* a heart;
- Makes you want to join his *home team*!

—*Maria Annette Hornage*
Oakland, California

First, the ideal man is not perfect, and doesn't think he is. He can laugh at his mistakes and learn from them. He's comfortable in a pair of jeans, or a three-piece suit. He has that down-home sex appeal. If I had to spell it out:

M is for the magic he brings into my life

A is for the admirable qualities he lives by

N is for never, ever being abusive towards a woman or child.

—*Theresa J. McClendon*
Cincinnati, Ohio

*H*e has:

- the physical ability to embrace without confining
- the emotional ability to comfort without controlling
- the spiritual ability to lead without demanding
- the social ability to organize, without dictating
- the ability to share ideas, yet not be argumentative
- the ability to express opinions, yet listen
- the ability to offer constructive criticism, yet encourage you to grow

———*Remona Wilson Winston*
Tuscaloosa, Alabama

*D*o you love with your heart?
Do you love with your mind?
Look beyond my exterior
Is there beauty still that you find?
Can you respect me?
Can you be true?
Not only to me, but also to you?
Are you passionate?
Are you strong?
Can you hold me close all night long?
'Cause when I find you and you find me
This is exactly the kind of man I hope you to be.

———*Xzenia B. Wilson*
Vallejo, California

To Make People Love You

Take nine lumps of starch, nine of sugar, nine teaspoons of steel dust. Wet it all with Jockey Club cologne. Take nine pieces of ribbon, blue, red or yellow. Take a dessertspoonful and put it on a piece of ribbon and tie it in a bag. As each fold is gathered together call his name. As you wrap it with yellow thread call his name till you finish. Make nine bags and place them under a rug, behind an armoire, under a step or over a door. They will love you and give you everything they can get. Distance makes no difference. Your mind is talking to his mind and nothing beats that.

Zora Neale Hurston

Dream Lover

I don't see him as often now
my imagination has given way
to more practical pursuits
but every now and again
he finds me
and I'm staring into his eyes
and I obey my resilient heart
his eyes are a prelude to his absolute beauty
they scream above our reticence
and in that moment he provides me total
trust and honesty
and I offer him myself
his understanding is a sign of his respect
he looks like poetry to me
like I could peel back layer upon layer
and find meanings heavier than his stare
like Black poetry
'cause just when I think I can pinpoint his beauty
the words for it change and I'm left holding his shadow
and the lean brown arms he offered
a minute ago are sometimes all I capture
and I know that given all I've experienced
I'm still not afraid to dream

—*Alison A. Cross*
Fremont, California

Visionary: unafraid of the winds of change that beat
steadily at his door, using each change
as an opportunity for success.

Builder: like an ant who builds its community, he
works in harmony with others.

Lover: whose ways are like gentle rain, meeting
the needs of his partner.

Protector: like the lion watching over her pride when
an enemy is approaching.

One who dares to be free.

— *Carol J. Queener*
Youngstown, Ohio

The musical yearnings of my heart give vivid color to my
visions, awakening my knowledge of he who has captured
my soul, yet set me free.

I am Mother, Sister, Lover to whomever I acknowledge as
the ideal man.

— *Linda Taylor-Musgrove*
College Park, Maryland

The Dream

sparkling eyes

sensual arms

powerful legs

a carefree laugh

a confident grin

a perfect walk

a warm embrace

a lively sense of humor

a loving touch

passionate kisses

a spontaneous romantic

never-ending patience

continuous understanding

a strong devotion to God

tender honesty

a gentle heart

deeply respectful

a calming strength

a life with a purpose

a man with whom my soul can run naked

—*Pamela Y. Flynn*
Richmond, Virginia

A description of my ideal man must begin with a good look inside rather than at the physical attributes with which he greets the world.

Does he have a strong spiritual center from which springs integrity, sensitivity and moral character?

Does he know and appreciate who he is, the legacy of his past, and does he have a vision for the future?

Does he have the ability to laugh with me, cry with me and stay with me when circumstances seem to dictate that he should shout, fight and flee?

Does he know that he is blessed?

—*Regina G. Sherard*
Decatur, Georgia

*H*ead held high with the greatest of confidence.
As you take great strides, it reveals your pride.
Strong hands, yet tender touch.
A smile to warm the coldest of hearts.
A take charge kind of man,
But not domineering or seeking control.
Sensitivity to cry,
Which makes you no less the ideal guy.

—*Amorette Milburn*
Philadelphia, Pennsylvania

*A*dmits it when he blows it;
Has a relationship with God;
Honors his parents;
Works hard for himself and his family;
Is a good listener;
Agrees to disagree;
Forgives;
Enjoys his own company;
Has goals and gradually accomplishes them;
Is affectionate, considerate and able to stand his ground;
Knows how to have fun;
Unashamed of his history;
Believes the sky is the limit!
Enjoys children and doesn't abuse his power.

—Robin Dawn
Seattle, Washington

He starts each day with a prayer and ends it with a "thank you Lord." This man is not easily influenced or intimidated, nor is he insecure. He holds you firmly when you cry and gently when he makes love to you. He loves to be pampered and loves to pamper back.

He often says "we," loves his family and tolerates mine. This man knows his limitations and feels no less a man because of them.

—Iris Washington
Pontiac, Michigan

Sea Lyric

Over the seas to-night, love,
  Over the darksome deeps,
Over the seas to-night, love,
  Slowly my vessel creeps.
Over the seas to-night, love,
  Waking the sleeping foam--
Sailing away from thee, love,
  Sailing from thee and home.
Over the seas to-night, love,
  Dreaming beneath the stars--
Till in my dreams you shine, love,
  Bright as the listening stars.

William Stanley Braithwaite
1908

The ideal man will embrace you when you need holding, release you when you need space, come when you call, give help when you need it, stand his ground when you're wrong and apologize when he is, ask your opinion, respect you, appreciate you, complement you, and share his dreams with you while learning about your dreams.

The ideal man is not perfect, and he doesn't need to be. He is faithful and honest... and available.

—*Rosalyn R. Skinner*
Fort Worth, Texas

The silent yearnings of my heart draw colorless visions through my mind and outline who he is:

Father: Thoughtful, Heroic, Experienced.

Brother: Intelligent, Dedicated, Egalitarian, Ambitious, Logical, and

Lover: Planted Mellow, Grown Aware, and Harvested Noble.

—*Linda Taylor-Musgrove*
College Park, Maryland

In touch with his soul.
Uncontrolled by addictions.

Knows God... follows His direction.
Compassionate,
Unafraid to show affection.
A planner who follows through.
Manages his finances.

Works when working.
Playful when playing.
Can listen to a woman
And hear what she is saying.

Capable of original thought,
Knows when to follow,
When to be boss.
Can cook if he needs to,
Clean when necessary... .

A man,
Who'd plan
A romantic getaway
On Super Bowl Sunday... .

—*Brynndah Hicks Turnbo*
Dallas, Texas

My Ideal Man Is Someone:

Who loves and respects his mother;
Who believes in his own race of women,
    desiring no other;
Who knows his own manhood,
    not questioning whether he's one way or the other;
Who works hard for his dollar,
    be he educated or blue collar;
Who can stand responsibility;
Who is— or can be— a good, loving caring, fatherly man;
Who is family oriented and enjoys life;
Who does not mind lending a helping hand;
Who loves me dearly.

          — *Carol J. Willams*
          Reynoldsburg, Ohio

The ideal man is the embodiment of the alphabet of life. He is: *A*ffectionate, has a *B*oyish charm, *C*ompetent, *D*ependable, not *E*gotistical, a true *F*riend, *G*entle, *H*ard-working, unintimidated by *I*ntimacy, *J*ovial, *K*indhearted, can *L*augh at himself, *M*asculine and monogamous, *N*urturing, *O*ptimistic, *P*assionate, *Q*uotable, *R*omantic, deeply *S*piritual, *T*ender, *U*ndaunted by adversity, has a *V*ariety of interests, seeks *W*isdom continually, not a *X*erox copy, *Y*outhful in mind and spirit, and has a *Z*est for life.

          — *Anita Snow*
          Tualatin, Florida

Fourteen

Short and Sweet
Great One-Liners

A collage of short entries capturing Black women's vision of the ideal man is contained in the following pages. You will recognize most of these passages— they are one-line excerpts from reflections in earlier chapters. Some passages represent new voices that add extra flavor.

Frequently tender, sometimes sweet, and occasionally sassy, these passages are sure to please!

*I*nstead of "the ideal man," I want "a deal man": a man who keeps up his end of the deal, whatever deal was made.

— *Sharon Harris*
Norcross, Georgia

*H*e makes love with the passion of a raging storm, and calls my name during the power of his "thunder."

—*Gloria J. McGibony*
Cocoa, Florida

*L*oves his mother, and fears my brothers.

—*Joilaina Diane Walters*
Cocoa, Florida

*M*y ideal man embodies those qualities I love and cherish in my closest women friends, only clothed with his own distinct male energy.

—*Denise L. McIver*
Los Angeles, California

*H*is personality should be like a Seafood Gumbo, with a variety of all good stuff.

—*Michelle A. Moore*
Elizabeth, New Jersey

*H*e knows what continent Egypt is on!

—*Brenda Moss Muhummad*
San Francisco, California

*Q*uite simply, the ideal man is perfectly imperfect, dependably independent and madly in love with me.

—*Cheryl Williams*
Middletown, New York

*S*omeone who isn't intimidated by my strength and independence but who embraces and encourages it.

—*Joan Finley*
Hillside, Illinois

The ideal man is intimately aware that there is a power greater than himself guiding all things.

—*Afrika Afeni Mills*
Brighton, Massachusetts

Sculptured arms and chest, thighs hard and strong, and a butt so tight and firm you just have to have a hand-full.

—*Elaine Paige*
Westland, Michigan

He knows that he is *the man* but he does not have an abusive bone in his body.

—*Wanda P. Payton*
Baltimore, Maryland

The ideal man lives with a clear conscience, a calm spirit, and a "saved" soul.

—*Karen S. Waugh*
Columbus, Ohio

He understands that true intimacy begins in the living room and not the bedroom.

—*Carla O' Brien and Fran Henry*
Brooklyn, New York

He has to have a spiritual background, be independent and not live in his mom's basement.

—*Robin Norman*
Philadelphia, Pennsylvania

He's cordial to your family, even if he hates their guts.

—*Anna Reeves*
Columbia, South Carolina

A man who lets you know he feels blessed to have you.

—*Sherrill D. Scott*
Yonkers, New York

His walk says, "I have been trying and will continue."

—*Hazel Wilson*
Mt. Vernon, New York

He is soft when he loves me, and hard when he protects me.

—*Janine B. Smith*
Lincoln Park, Michigan

A God-fearing man who knows how much value a woman can add to his life.

—*Kimberly Jimson*
Rialto, California

He is receptive to learning new things and wants to make a change.

—*Jarika L. Blizzard*
Hampton, Virginia

He encourages me to be all of who I am, while giving all of who he is.

—*Ida R. Ivey*
Tulsa, Oklahoma

The man takes the time to get to know you before he gets to *knnooww yoouu!*

—*Tiffany Griffin*
Washington, D.C.

He would view life optimistically because he knows that although there are some rough times, joy always comes in the morning.

—*Tina Walker*
Indianapolis, Indiana

*H*e loves your children and lets them know that he's genuinely interested in them— not just their mother.

—*Mary Greene-blade*
Ruston, Louisiana

*H*e takes a stand, even if he's the only one standing.

—*Marria Bratcher*
Oklahoma City, Oklahoma

*H*e has the defiance of your first teen attraction and the raw sexual magnetism of your lover.

—*Yvette Cordova-Sital*
Bronx, New York

*H*e is a virtuous and spiritual brother with a positive outlook and scintillating eyes that look only at me.

—*Jannyé W. Strickland*
Marrero, Louisiana

*T*he ideal man is one who teaches me any of life's lessons at any particular point in my life.

—*Rene Noreen Rawls*
Atlanta, Georgia

He trusts that I won't cheat and I know he wouldn't dare.

—Jennifer F. Bogar
Newark, New Jersey

The man who loves you despite your past, because of your present, and with hope for your shared future.

—Penelope Luster-Downs
Lincoln, Nebraska

He is a mature man, not simply a person who has aged.

—Loretta Allison
Temple Hills, Maryland

He's brave enough to tell me when he's too weak to finish the race.

—Angel M. James
Istanbul, Turkey

Willing to accept me as his full-figured woman, and climbing the highest mountain top to shout to the world that I am his woman!

—Saundra A. Giles
Warner Robins, Georgia

The ideal man will embrace you when you need holding, release you when you need space and come when you call.

—*Rosalyn R. Skinner*
Fort Worth, Texas

A heterosexual— I have no desire to compete with "Bill" for his attention.

—*Chyrille P. McIntosh*
Miramar, Florida

He is a man who can appreciate the pleasure of sharing a starry night or a breathless sunset.

—*Sharron McDonald*
Durham, North Carolina

Living with respect, calm, perseverance; he amuses, pleases, gets the job done.

—*Tia Hairston-Edwards*
New Haven, Connecticut

One who stops at nothing to tell me how precious I am to him, who tells me I am his jewel of inestimable value.

—*Grace Ilonuba*
Riverdale, Georgia

The ideal man could love this woman forever, making marriage the only answer.

— *Salundia Yarbough*
Ypsilanti, Michigan

He yearns for the simple moments in a relationship that include hugs that say, "I believe in you and I know you believe in me."

—*Renee Rolling*
Chamblee, Georgia

The ideal man will know how to handle going to bed one night next to a coke-bottle-figured woman and waking up to a woman with a milk-jug body.

—*Jacqueline Lenore Hollingsworth*
Dallas, Texas

He loves this child-bearing, baby-carrying-hips, sit-a-TV-on-it-butt, breast-giving-in-to-gravity body of mine.

—*Tara Hogan*
North Hollywood, California

*H*is life experiences have made him better not bitter; whole, not fragmented.

—*JoAnn Scott*
Paterson, New Jersey

I am looking for an all-grown-up, ain't-scared-of-nuthin', and know-it's-time-to-save-the-race man.

—*Leonia Collins*
Marietta, Georgia

*M*y ideal man is my best friend, has a "j-o-b" and files a W-2 yearly.

—*Katrina Lawrence-Martin*
Rome, Georgia

*H*is heart holds the boundless love of a considerate, compassionate man.

—*Rogena Walden*
Cartersville, Georgia

A man whose only regret in life is that he didn't find you sooner.

—*Amie M. Morehead*
Washington, D.C.

The ideal man knows and realizes that his erections are not his main source of manhood.

— *Sonia Watson*
Houston, Texas

In truth, every jewel has its flaw but a man who seeks peace and balance through a Higher Power is perfection regardless.

—*Jamilla Coleman*
Atlanta, Georgia

He deals with the good and the bad, especially if he decides to say "I do."

—*JoWanna Etheridge*
Birmingham, Alabama

This is definitely a man who can satisfy his mate a complete lifetime, without chasing other women... after all, any "dog" can and will do that.

—*Bennie Prince*
Vancouver, Washington

*A*s he speaks, you can sense intelligence, passion and honesty indicating that he is always ready to compromise.

—*Jerri Sherrod*
Chicago, Illinois

*L*ove is a two-way street and he is not afraid to do some walking.

—*Anastasia McGahee*
Chicago, Illinois

*T*he man my parents prayed I'd find.

—*Carmen Avery*
Birmingham, Alabama

A man you can really call "friend," a friend you can truly call "lover," and a being gifted enough to qualify as both.

—*Amie M. Morehead*
Washington, D.C.

*H*e has east coast work ethics, west coast ideas, and southern values!

—*Nuria*
Chicago, Illinois

I know there is absolutely nothing as profound as a man who uses the gift of common sense.

—*Valerie D. Parker*
Richmond, Virginia

A manchild born of the struggle, unafraid of the battle, wanting to win, able to love.

—*Dabura Karriem*
Brooklyn, New York

He's willing to let me spread my wings and fly, knowing that I'd never fly too far away from his life.

—*Isadora Coger*
Charleston, South Carolina

*L*oves my dog but never dogged a female.

—*E. K. Daufin*
Montgomery, Alabama

He understands downfalls are only stepping stones, not brick walls.
—*Pearl G. Bailey*
Bronx, New York

A man who doesn't have to figure me out like I'm a "1,000 piece jigsaw puzzle."

—*Karla L. Wasson*
Detroit, Michigan

A man who'd plan a romantic getaway on Super Bowl Sunday.

—*Brynndah Hicks Turnbo*
Dallas, Texas

*T*he ideal man is one who is committed to me and a monogamous relationship.

—*Barbara E. Kinch*
Philadelphia, Pennsylvania

*H*e is a man who has a soul that connects to a heart which touches his mind to make him a human being with backbone.

—*Taylor Frances*
City & State Withheld

*H*e's strong enough to cry, but not weak enough to give up.

—*Lila Rometa Collins*
Memphis, Tennessee

A man who, when you're in his company, seems to make the world disappear.

——*Marcenda Ry*
New York, New York

*H*e doesn't have the most money in the world or the best looks, but he loves me and that's all that matters.

—— *Sonya M. Tarton*
Memphis, Tennessee

*T*ime to toss out the complex description of Mr. Right and be thankful for a level-headed brother with a job!

—— *Shelina Dawn Wallace*
Philadelphia, Pennsylvania

*H*e possesses quiet strength, giving his partner an innate feeling of peace and security.

——*Darneisha Airhart*
Fort Smith, Arkansas

A Black man who is compassionate, communicative, and possesses a spiritual base that connects him to his divinity.

—*Monica L. Johnson*
Reseda, California

Although his eye may roam, his body, mind and soul rest with one woman.

—*Dawn K. Guillory*
Lake Charles, Louisiana

He is secure enough to appreciate her essence and couples it with arms stretched to catch her if she falls.

—*Aginah Smart*
Philadelphia, Pennsylvania

Hypnotizing ebony eyes, a sense of humor and a job are an absolute must.

—*Lynn Morrow*
Fort Worth, Texas

Doesn't collect women like trophies on a shelf!

—*Chinyere Ahaghotu-Nwani*
Washington, DC

I believe the foundation on which the Black man stands is what will hold him up in the end.

— *Sandra Longstreet*
Toledo, Ohio

In his senior years, he will look at his woman and say, "you're as beautiful now as the first time I laid my eyes on you."

— *Bredget Powe*
Chesapeake, South Carolina

A man who can show his true emotions and leave the "macho front" in the backwoods.

— *Yolanda Brunson*
Brooklyn, New York

The ideal man is one you can respect.

— *Deborah Stinson-Melton*
Long Beach, California

Believes in his abilities and shares the belief that anything worth having is worth working and waiting for.

—*Monica Martin*
Riverside, California

He realizes the injustice of society, but does not allow himself to become a victim.

—*Bedie A. Steele*
Herndion, Virginia

Gently loving, confident enough to let sista be.

—*Deanna M. King*
Denver, Colorado

A great lover and cook!

—*Tashema R. Lindsey*
Chicago, Illinois

Features and looks are nice but there is nothing like a fit or flabby pair of biceps wrapped around a sister in her darkest hour.

—*Altha Thompson*
Chicago, Illinois

A hardworking, spiritual man, lacking nothing that properly belongs to him.

—*Robin A. Barlow*
New Orleans, Louisiana

He has two strong hands, one to hold you and the other to help carry your bags after a day of power shopping.

—*Deidrah Thomas*
Detroit, Michigan

He is willing to share his life with you, keeping nothing hidden.

—*Angela M. Citizen-Payne*
Hawthorne, California

He must be bold enough to stand and say, "I love the Lord," and also, "I love my woman."

—*Penny Denny*
East Spencer, North Carolina

Enhanced with a mature sense of humor, he has the passion to be a good person.

—*Valerie Y. Meekins*
Alexandria, Virginia

The ideal man is analogous to a good stock portfolio: diversified.

—*Marilyn S. Johnson-Henry*
Madison, Alabama

As I continue to take my life's journey, I have realized that love from Mr. Right can't be the blessing I desire if I do not have it within myself.

—*Beverly Canady*
Newark, New Jersey

The ideal man is a man who can see your flaws and your underdeveloped character, and love you in spite of it all.

— *Sheila L. Walker-Warner*
Columbus, Georgia

Good looks are a definite plus, but I'll choose depth and personality over well-honed looks any day.

—*Helen Jones*
Osceola, Arkansas

The ideal man must also know the difference between holding a hand and chaining a soul.

—*Janita F. Middleton*
Southfield, Michigan

He doesn't take kindness for weakness. This man knows the true meaning of love.

—*Gwendolyn Maxine Collins*
Milton, Massachusetts

A friend, a lover and someone who is not connected with an ex-love!

— *Selena M. Wade*
Yeadon, Pennsylvania

If You Enjoyed *All The Man I Need* ...

...You will love our next book, *Our Romantic Ways*. The authors of *All The Man I Need* are at it again, and they need your help. *Our Romantic Ways* will be the first book focusing on the creative and unique ways African Americans are romantic.

Our Romantic Ways will contain romantic suggestions that range from small gestures such as writing love poetry to more elaborate surprises such as planning a romantic getaway for your love. Get the idea? This is where you come in. We want to hear stories of the most romantic things anyone has ever done for you, the most romantic thing you have ever done for anyone else, or your ideas about great romantic gestures from your own imagination. We are interested in more than the standard gestures such as sending flowers and eating out.

We are excited about *Our Romantic Ways* and we are sure it will become the definitive guide for romance for African-Americans. The emphasis here is on ROMANCE, and we would love to hear from both Women and Men. Please limit your entry to 100 words or less.

If we use your story or idea, we will send you a free copy of the finished book. You have the option of being acknowledged as a contributor or remaining anonymous. Just let us know in your letter. Please note that all material submitted will be the property of Gateway Publishers. No further permission is required for the company to edit and use it by any form, printed or electronic, to promote romance in the Black community.

Send your submissions: Our Romantic Ways
                            Gateway Publishers
                            P.O. Box 1749
                            Newark, NJ 07101

Fifteen

Partner Assessment and
Compatibility Test (PACT™)
A Test To Find Out If He Is Worthy Of You

The Partner Assessment and Compatibility Test or PACT™ is a test designed to help you determine if your current or prospective partner is ideal for you.

The PACT questions reflect the collective wisdom of the 1,850 women who entered the "Mr. Right" Contest in which women were invited to write about the type of men they want in their lives. The issues addressed in the test touch upon the items most frequently mentioned by the women who sent us their submissions. Ranked according to how frequently the attributes were mentioned, women said they find appealing men who:

1. are spiritual or religious;
2. are kind, gentle, compassionate, and sensitive;
3. have strong characters and are dignified;
4. are honest, faithful, and committed;
5. are romantic, sexy, sensual, and good lovers;

6. comfort, pamper, and protect;
7. respect women and treat their mothers right;
8. love women as they are and are non-controlling;
9. are family oriented; and
10. have a sense of humor.

The PACT is divided into seven sections designed to gauge most of the attributes listed above. The seventh section, Negative Qualities, is designed to identify negative or destructive attributes that can make a potentially ideal man, not so ideal. We have assumed that items in this Negative Qualities section are not so destructive that they completely disqualify a male candidate from consideration.

However, many of the women who responded to the "Mr. Right" Contest felt that some negative attributes should disqualify a candidate or, at least, should cause a woman to strongly reconsider the relationship. They considered the following qualities to be destructive to a relationship: physical and mental abuse, the desire for absolute control of a partner's behavior, extreme jealousy, substance abuse, addiction to an activity such as gambling, and habitual infidelity. If any of these conditions apply to your candidate, don't bother taking the test. The candidate has already failed— for now. Of course, we know that when it comes to human behavior, there is always room for redemption. If a man is seriously seeking help for his problems, there is hope. But these negative attributes are warning signals that should not be ignored under any circumstances.

The test is designed to be completed by women who have a current partner or, at least, a candidate in mind. They are to assess the qualities of their man as he is now, not as they would like him to be.

Because we believe that time reveals all personality flaws, the result of the test is more meaningful if you have known the candidate for six months or more. If you have known him for less than six months, take the test now, but repeat it again when you know him a little better.

For now, sit back, relax and let's examine the man!

PARTNER ASSESSMENT & COMPATIBILITY TEST
(PACT™)

1. Spirituality
Circle The Appropriate Number
0 = never; 1 = rarely; 2 = sometimes; 3 = often; 4 = always

He believes he is answerable to a   0 1 2 3 4
higher power. *(Scoring example: if he
does not believe that he has to account
to God for his actions, choose "0".)*

He prays, meditates, or reads a   0 1 2 3 4
Holy Book (Bible, Koran, etc.)

A. Add Up Points and Place Total Here _____

2. Sensitivity
Circle The Appropriate Number
0 = never; 1 = rarely; 2 = sometimes; 3 = often; 4 = always

He is communicative &   0 1 2 3 4
shares his feelings with you

He listens and has an open ear   0 1 2 3 4
for your concerns, problems

He has compassion for others   0 1 2 3 4

He is honest   0 1 2 3 4

He has a sense of humor   0 1 2 3 4

B. Add Up Points & Place Total Here _____

3. Strength In Character

Circle The Appropriate Number
0 = never; 1 = rarely; 2 = sometimes; 3 = often; 4 = always

He is intelligent   0 1 2 3 4

He is street smart   0 1 2 3 4

He has common sense   0 1 2 3 4

He is ambitious   0 1 2 3 4

He is African-centered or   0 1 2 3 4
shows pride in his
cultural heritage

He is community minded   0 1 2 3 4
(Does he give something back?)

He has high self-esteem &   0 1 2 3 4
confidence

He is financially independent   0 1 2 3 4

He is mature   0 1 2 3 4

His life experiences have made   0 1 2 3 4
him better, not bitter

He is taking steps to improve   0 1 2 3 4
himself by going to school,
taking classes, etc.

C. Add Points Up & Place Total Here   _____

4. Respect
Circle The Appropriate Number
0 = never; 1 = rarely; 2 = sometimes; 3 = often; 4 = always

He respects women	0 1 2 3 4
He respects his mother	0 1 2 3 4
He encourages your independence	0 1 2 3 4
He encourages your success	0 1 2 3 4
He respects your intelligence	0 1 2 3 4
He recognizes that you add value to the quality of his life	0 1 2 3 4

D. Add Up Points & Place Total Here _____

5. Ability To Pamper, Protect, & Provide
Circle The Appropriate Number
0 = never; 1 = rarely; 2 = sometimes; 3 = often; 4 = always

He pampers you especially when things in your life are going wrong	0 1 2 3 4
He remembers days that are special to you (birthdays, etc.)	0 1 2 3 4

E. Add Up Points & Place Total Here _____

6. Romance

Circle The Appropriate Number
0 = never; 1 = rarely; 2 = sometimes; 3 = often; 4 = always

He makes sure you are satisfied sexually	0 1 2 3 4
He accepts friendship first before sex	0 1 2 3 4
He wants a commitment	0 1 2 3 4
He has good hygiene	0 1 2 3 4
He is a skilled lover	0 1 2 3 4
He is intimate in bed without asking for sex	0 1 2 3 4
You are satisfied with his looks, body, and whole appearance	0 1 2 3 4
His charm and wit turn you on	0 1 2 3 4
He overlooks your physical imperfections	0 1 2 3 4
He makes you feel beautiful (even if you don't believe you are)	0 1 2 3 4
He demonstrates how much he cares for you by his behavior or his gestures.(Flowers, poetry, picking you up from work, etc.)	0 1 2 3 4
He is willing to compromise	0 1 2 3 4

F. Add Up Points & Place Total Here _____

7. Negative Qualities
Circle The Appropriate Number
0 = never; 1 = rarely; 2 = sometimes; 3 = often; 4 = always

He expects his lover to fully support him financially. *(Scoring Example: If he always expects his lover to support him financially, he would rate a "4" in this category.)*	0 1 2 3 4
He is a selfish lover. He is more concerned about his sexual satisfaction than yours.	0 1 2 3 4
He has high credit card debt or bad credit incurred by an extravagant lifestyle	0 1 2 3 4
He has no desire to improve himself	0 1 2 3 4
He lets family members run his life	0 1 2 3 4
He is intimidated by your strength	0 1 2 3 4
He is intimidated by your success	0 1 2 3 4
He is intimidated by your intelligence	0 1 2 3 4
He uses racism as an excuse to do nothing for himself	0 1 2 3 4

G. Add Up Points & Place Total Here _____

SCORING

Basic Instructions

Step 1   Add up all points from lines A, B, C, D, E, and F in the first 5 Sections: Spirituality; Sensitivity; Strength In Character; Respect; Ability To Pamper, Protect , & Provide; and Romance.

Step 2   Multiply the number of points on line G by 2.

Step 3   Subtract the balance calculated in Step 2 from balance calculated in Step 1

Example

Points from Line A = 5

Points from Line B = 10

Points from Line C = 30

Points from Line D = 20

Points from Line E = 8

Points from Line F = 34

Points from Line G = 4

Step 1 $A+B+C+D+E+F = 5+10+30+20+8+34 = 107$

Step 2 $G \times 2 = 4 \times 2 = 8$

Step 3   Step 1 - Step 2 = 107 - 8 = 99

Assessment Of Score	
Below 100	Mr. Wrong
100 to 120	Mr. So So
121 to 140	Mr. Right
Above 140	Mr. Perfect

Sixteen

Demographics and Analysis
Age Distribution | Marital Status
Geographical Distribution | Rank Of Important Qualities

This chapter takes a closer look at the 1,850 women who entered the "Mr. Right" Contest. It ranks, by percentage, the top 10 qualities that the women who responded to the contest look for in their men. In addition, it provides information about the ages, the marital status, and the geographical distribution of the entrants to the contest.

Based on the entries we received, we put together a list (Table 1) of the 10 most desired qualities the women indicated that they look for in men.

TABLE 1

Qualities Sought By Women According To Their Entries	% Of Women* Who Mentioned Qualities In Their Entries
1. Spirituality and Religious Convictions.	35%
2. Kindness, Gentleness, Compassion, and Sensitivity.	34%
3. Strength In Character and Dignity Despite Indignities.	26%
4. Honesty, Faithfulness, and Commitment.	26%
5. Sensuality and Romance (Including Unselfishness In Lovemaking).	21%
6. Ability To Pamper, Comfort, and Protect.	21%
7. Respect For Women (Especially Their Mother). Not Abusive.	20%
8. A Non-controlling Nature, An Unconditional Lover.	16%
9. Family Oriented.	15%
10. A Sense of Humor.	13%

*Percentages Add Up To More Than 100 Because The Women Mentioned Multiple Personality Qualities In Their Entries

Spirituality, mentioned in 35% of the entries, dominated the list of qualities that Black women look for in a man. In general, the women considered Spirituality to be an indispensable shield to help partners withstand life's difficulties. In their view, because a spiritual man knows he is answerable to God for his behavior, he is more likely to act responsibly than a non-spiritual man.

While Spirituality reigns supreme, a kind, gentle, and compassionate man is a very close second (34% of the entries).

Make no mistake about it, these women are not looking for a doormat or a wimp. Strength in character and confidence are a real turn-on for 26% of the entrants, especially when directed toward maintaining one's dignity and sticking to one's principles during hard times. However, many of the women emphasize that they can do without the "macho front."

Next on the list is honesty, faithfulness, and commitment (26% of the entries). As one woman put it, she wants a man who "keeps up his end of the deal, whatever deal was made."

An unselfish lover (21% of the entries) is highly desirable. A man that 1) can provide romantic and tender moments outside of the bedroom and, 2) as one women wrote, make love "with the passion of a raging storm," seems to be a winning combination.

Pampering, comforting, and in general, providing a shoulder to lean on are highly valued by 21% of the woman who responded to the contest.

A man who listens to and respects women is certainly admired (20% of the entries). Many women mentioned that the key to finding out whether a man respects women is to observe how he treats his mother. In their opinion, if he treats his mother with love and respect, there's a good chance that he will treat his woman similarly.

Next on the list, is a man who does not try to change or control his partner (16% of the entries). As one woman put it, the man must "know the difference between holding a hand, and chaining a soul."

Fifteen percent of the women wrote that a family man is also highly valued. As expressed by one entrant, she wants someone who "takes care of his children from diapers to diplomas." Others wrote of their desire for a man who would be a good role model for their children. Furthermore, in an age where people acquire ready-made families upon entering relationships, it is understandable why many women indicated that a man must be willing to take on the responsibility of raising children that are not his own.

A man with a sense of humor is very important to 13% of the entrants. For these women, a sense of humor helps both partners weather the ups and downs in a relationship. And, as one woman wrote, "Humor keeps your life expectancy up, stress down, puts a positive glow on your face, and illuminates your soul."

A breakdown of the ages of the women who submitted passages for the "Mr. Right" Contest is shown on Table 2.

TABLE 2

Age Category	% In Age Categories
16 to 21	7%
22-27	25%
28-33	31%
34-39	17%
40-45	15%
Over 45	5%

The median age of the entrants was 32. The youngest and the oldest entrant was 16 and 72 respectively.

Table 3 shows the marital status of the entrants.

TABLE 3

Marital Status	% In Each Category
Single	70%
Married	15%
Divorced	12%
Separated	2%
Widowed	1%

Geographically, the women who entered the contest came from 40 states and from overseas. Table 4 shows the 20 states that contributed about 88% of the entrants, while the balance of the entrants came from another 20 states not identified in the table.

TABLE 4

States	% From Each State
New York	14%
California	8%
Georgia	7%
Illinois	6%
Pennsylvania	5%
Maryland	5%
Ohio	5%
Michigan	5%
Florida	4%
Texas	4%
New Jersey	4%
North Carolina	4%
Virginia	3%
Alabama	3%
South Carolina	2%
Tennessee	2%
Massachusetts	2%
Missouri	2%
Connecticut	2%
Louisiana	1%
20 Other States	12%

APPENDIX

INDEX OF NAMES

BIBLIOGRAPHY AND PERMISSIONS

Chapter One: HAKI R. MADHUBUTI: "To the Men and Women," *HeartLove: Wedding and Love Poems*, Copyright 1998 by Haki R. Madhubuti, reprinted by permission of Third Wold Press, Inc., Chicago, Illinois. Chapter Two: LIZELIA AUGUSTA JENKINS MOORER: "Whisper Words of Love To Me", *Prejudice Unveiled and Other Poems* (first printing Boston, Mass: Roxburgh Publishing Company, 1907, p. 107)(The Schomburg Library of 19th Century Black Women Writers, New York, New York: The Oxford University Press, 1988, v. 3, p. 107). Chapter Three: "Nwanyibuife", *Womanbeing & African Literature* edited by Phanuel A. Egejuru and Ketu H. Katrak (Trenton, NJ: First African World Press, 1997, p. 11) by permission of the publisher. W.E.B. DUBOIS: "Woman Suffrage", *The Crisis*, November, 1915. Chapter Four: "How the Ethiopian Woman Tamed Her Husband", *African Voices: The First Anthology of Native African Writing* compiled and edited by Peggy Rutherford (New York, New York: The Vanguard Press, Inc. pp. 69 - 70). HAKI R. MADHUBUTI: "The Union of Two," *HeartLove:: Wedding and Love Poems*, Copyright 1998 by Haki R. Madhubuti, reprinted by permission of Third Wold Press, Inc., Chicago, Illinois.reprinted from *HeartLove: Wedding and Love Poems* (Chicago, Illinois: Third Wold Press, 1998) with permission of the author. Chapter Six: ALICE RUTH MOORE DUNBAR-NELSON: "The Woman", *Violets and Other Tales*, (Boston, Mass.: Monthly Review Press, 1895, 1898, p. 27). MABEL DOVE-DANQUAH: "Anticipation". *Daughters of Africa: An International Anthology of Words and Writings by Women of African Descent From the Ancient Egyptian to the Present* edited by Margaret Busby (New York, New York: Ballantine Books, 1995, p.225). Chapter Seven: GEORGE MOSES HORTON: "George Moses Horton: Slave Poet", Stephen B. Weeks, *Southern Workman*, October, 1914. MARY WESTON FORDHAM: Lines to _____", *Magnolia Leaves: Poems by Mary Weston Fordham With An Introductory by Booker T. Washington* (first published Tuskeegee, Alabama: 1897, p. 68*)* (The Schomburg Library of 19th Century Black Women Writers, New York, New York: The Oxford University Press, 1988, v. 2, p. 68). Chapter Eight: PAUL LAURENCE DUNBAR: "Invitation to Love", *Lyrics of Lowly Life* (London, England: Chapman & Hall, Ltd., 1897). JAMES WELDON JOHNSON: "Nobody's Lookin But De Owl and De Moon", *Fifty Years & Other Poems* (Boston, Mass: Cornhill Company, 1917). Chapter Nine: ZORA NEALE HURSTON: "Love", *Dust Tracks on a Road* copyright 1942 by Zora Neale Hurston, renewed 1970 by John C. Hurston (Zora Neale Hurston: *Folklore, Memoirs, And Other Writings*. New York: The Library of America, 1995). JOSEPHINE HENDERSON HEARD: "My Husband's Birthday", *Morning Glories* (The Schomburg Library of 19th Century Black Women Writers, New York, New York: The Oxford University Press, 1988, p. 42). Chapter Ten: TERRICK HAMILTON: *Antar, A Bedoueen Romance* (translated from the Arabic)(London, England: John Murray 1820). PAUL LAURENCE DUNBAR: "A Negro Love Song", *Lyrics of Lowly Life* (London, England: Chapman & Hall, Ltd., 1897). Chapter 11. *Families and Freedom: A Documentary History of African-American Kinship in the Civil War Era* edited by Ira Berlin and Leslie S. Rowland (New York, New York: The New York Press, 1997), pp. 196 - 197. *Selections From The Husia:: Sacred Wisdom of Ancient Egypt* selected and retranslated by Maulana Karenga (Los Angeles, Calif.: Kawaida Publications, 1995, p. 58). Chapter 13: ZORA NEALE HURSTON, *Mules and Men*, copyright 1935 by Zora Neale Hurston. Renewed 1963 by John C. Hurston and Joel Hurston (New York, New York: Harper & Row, Publishers, 1935) p. 276. WILLIAM STANLEY BRAITHWAITE: "Sea Lyric", *Lyrics of Life and Love*, (Boston, Mass. : Herbert B. Turner & Co., 1904).

```
┌─────────────────────────────────────────────────────┐
│                                                       │
│        ORDERING FROM GATEWAY PUBLISHERS              │
│                                                       │
│   All The Man I Need: Black Women's Loving Expressions On The │
│   Men They Desire by Anaezi Modu and Andrea Walker is │
│   available from Gateway Publishers at special discounts for │
│   bulk purchases for sales promotions, premiums, fund-raising, │
│   or educational use.                                 │
│                                                       │
│   To order individual copies, please send $15.95 plus $3.75 for │
│   shipping and handling. Checks should be made out to Gate- │
│   way Publishers and sent to the following address:   │
│                                                       │
│              Gateway Publishers (EM)                  │
│                  P.O. Box 1749                        │
│                Newark, NJ 07101                       │
│                 1-800-511-2394                        │
│                                                       │
└─────────────────────────────────────────────────────┘
```

See Page 227 If You Want To Be Part Of Our Next Book:

Our Romantic Ways
By
Anaezi Modu & Andrea Walker

Please Visit Anaezi Modu's and Andrea Walker's Website

www.blackromantic.com